TEARS OF AN INNOCENT GOD

TEARS OF AN INNOCENT GOD

Conversations on Silence, Kindness, and Prayer

ELIAS MARECHAL

Paulist Press
New York / Mahwah, NJ

Cover image by Angela Waye / Shutterstock.com
Cover design by Sharyn Banks
Book design by Lynn Else

Elements of this book appeared in *Dancing Madly Backwards: A Journey into God* published by The Crossroad Publishing Company, New York. Copyright © 1982 by Elias Marechal.

Library of Congress Cataloging-in-Publication Data

Marechal, Paul.
    Tears of an innocent God : conversations on silence, kindness, and prayer / Elias Marechal.
        pages cm
    ISBN 978-0-8091-4939-1 (pbk. : alk. paper) — ISBN 978-1-58768-530-9 (ebook)
    1. Spiritual life—Christianity. I. Title.
    BV4501.3.M2575 2015
    248.4—dc23

                                                            2015009373

ISBN 978-0-8091-4939-1 (paperback)
ISBN 978-1-58768-530-9 (e-book)

Published by Paulist Press
997 Macarthur Boulevard
Mahwah, New Jersey 07430

www.paulistpress.com

Printed and bound in the
United States of America

Dedicated to
Alyce O'Brien
and
Joan Kajcienski
and
all the Afflicted of the Earth

Contents

Foreword by Emilie Griffin xi

Acknowledgments xv

Introduction: An Invitation to Conversation..................xvii

The First Conversation:
Of Silence, Kindness, and Prayer 1
   1. The Round Dance of the Trinity 3
   2. The Silence at the Bottom of the Soul........................9
   3. Rambling at Ease 15
   4. Contemplation in the Grotto 20
   5. When Dialogue Disappears......................................23
   6. The Power of His Name...27
   7. The Second Heart 31
   8. Praying with Gentle Strength..................................41
   9. The Beggar's Final Words...43
   Practice: The Prayer of Gratitude 45

The Second Conversation:
The Tears of an Innocent God 51
   1. The Radiant Christ 53
   2. The Tears of an Innocent God 57
   3. When God's Ways Seem Irrational............................60
   4. Conversing with God without Armor 65
   5. If Your Attention Wanders.....................................70

CONTENTS

6. And God Spoke 73

7. The Word Carries Us Wherever We Go 76

8. Christ, Imagination and the Gospels.............78

Practice: Imagination in Scripture...............83

The Third Conversation:

Tales Heard at Low Tide..............................**87**

1. Moshe 89

2. A Dream 94

3. A Christ of the Soul 99

4. The Little House 104

5. As the Angel of Death Drew Near 109

6. The Slave Cemetery 114

7. The Grand Silence 119

8. Under a Bridge in South Carolina 125

9. Gone, Yet Not Away.............................131

10. Another Dream................................134

Practice: Centering Prayer.......................137

The Fourth Conversation:

A Journey Waiting to Begin **141**

1. Into the Land of Likeness 143

2. A Yearning to Unfold...........................148

3. Honoring Our Uniqueness 151

4. The Prez 153

5. Dream with Both Eyes Open 155

6. What Have You Done with Your Life?.............160

7. The Last Dance.................................165

Practice: Seeing through Our Thoughts............171

The Fifth Conversation:

All I Ask Is that You Listen **177**

1. A Blessing or a Curse..........................179

2. Faces 183

3. An Image of Hope 187

Contents

4. A Blessing in Winter 191
5. Faith Is Fire, Not Sediment 196
6. A Sacred Song..200
7. The Music that Befriends Us.................................203
8. Why Not Become All Fire? 207
9. The Secret...211
Practice: Dealing with Afflictive Feelings 215

Foreword

When I first read *Tears of an Innocent God*, I had a sense of recognition. Here was the man, Paul Marechal, whom I had known since childhood. Now he was fully mature and formed by a lifelong service to Jesus Christ. His book, like his friendship, invited me more deeply into God's heart.

The man I knew has become older. He is Br. Elias Marechal, a Cistercian in the community at Conyers, Georgia. He freely shares—on these pages and when you meet him face-to-face—the fruit of his experience.

As a younger man, he traveled. His parents had given him a sense of being a world citizen, speaking several languages and influenced by many cultures. He went far and wide to know where he had come from and what his personal heritage might mean. He wanted to know what the wisdom of the past could offer.

But mostly he listened to God speaking in his heart. He felt a clear, insistent invitation and he followed that lead.

Now we who are his friends and readers are blessed by this account of his lifelong odyssey—for he has followed a constant and persistent call to come home.

Br. Elias traces a journey that is Homer's kind of voyage. It is ancient and familiar, old and new. But his pilgrimage is even more radical than that. Minute by minute, phrase by phrase, Br. Elias leads us into biblical truth.

Tears of an Innocent God records many insights that Br. Elias has gained from other writers. He cites the works of poets, ancient and modern, philosophers and thinkers, worldly and unworldly. But the thread of his journey never frays. The mooring-rope never gives way. Br. Elias wants us to understand personal transformation. He wants to lead us through that experience, not only his experience, but ours.

In that long-ago childhood I shared with Paul, I first learned about mystics and mysticism. I first learned that others —Paul was one of them—yearned for God as deeply as I did. In those days, I first began to grasp, dimly, that everyone felt a sense of displacement and loss, everyone wanted to transcend the challenges of living, everyone had questions without answers, desires of the broken heart. But it was many years—a lifelong odyssey of spiritual transformation—that called me homeward, back into the God-life I had sprung from, and to which I would return. Br. Elias—the Paul Marechal I knew long ago—has captured that yearning on these pages. Through stories and song, he helps us to reenter the world we have desired and thought we had lost forever, the world and life that were waiting for us all along.

Br. Elias is a man who understands the power of words and the Word. He knows prayer is more than mere utterance, but instead a deep relenting to God's heart, Christ's love, the Spirit-filled hope that leads us home.

Sometimes his stories are biblical. Sometimes they are Jesus stories. Sometimes they are stories that come out of a long wisdom tradition. Sometimes they float like Arctic and Antarctic shelves, unrooted, unsourced, unspecified on top of a vast, deep ocean of consciousness and remembering.

Tears of an Innocent God makes me grateful for a lifetime of estrangement and yearning. It makes me cherish every stone, every rock, and every boulder on the journey. It helps me to be healed by the loving heart of God, by the sweet surrender of Christ Jesus, and his companionship on the way.

And this is a book of instruction. Never mind that it isn't difficult or dry. The clear, simple structure and discipline of the spiritual life is made plain here. Br. Elias shows us the path, invites us to travel with Jesus and invoke his name. He plots the course, offers encouragement and correction. Marechal himself is so attuned to God's will and word for us that his words play a kind of melody that moves us on. Like Moses and Miriam crossing the Red Sea, he lifts the timbrel and urges us forward. More poet than professor, Marechal reminds us of the Lord's deep rhythm at the center of all events, soothing wounds, redeeming losses, comforting us for deprivations and regrets.

This odyssey is a healing journey. We are transformed by the music of God's love, his will for our lives to be made whole. Music, movement, poetry, storytelling, contemplation, prayer, all these are woven together in the mysterious odyssey that Br. Elias traces for us. He shows us how to receive the love of God. He shows us how to hold on when there are no answers, and there is only emptiness and waiting. Br. Elias understands the transforming power of trust. In all these ways, he is a master of the spiritual life.

If only we will listen, if we will enter into the silence, if we will pierce the noise and confrontation of things, if we will try a few steps, if we will let the silence change us, if we will let the power of consolation lift us up and over daunting challenges, if we will grasp an oar and row, not always wanting to command, and if we will move, soon we will feel the flow, the momentum. It is a journey of grace and peace. Even the portages will make us whole, and we will carry our loads with acceptance, even laughter, sometimes joy.

Can I capture in a single word or phrase what is most precious about this book? Doubtless I cannot and probably shouldn't try. Let the Lord Jesus lead you here. Begin. Turn the pages. Receive the healing sweetness of the Lord's presence. Go within, go deeper, go beyond. The Lord Himself is inviting you, and the voyage is amazing.

Emilie Griffin
August 2014
Alexandria, Louisiana USA

Acknowledgments

I am grateful to all who supported and encouraged me during the writing of this book. I am especially grateful to Martin Laird, Emilie Griffin, Carl McColman, Cynthia Johnson, Fr. Thomas Keating, Maria Lichtmann, Art Anderson, Paul McMahon, Fr. Anthony Delisi, Jack Moran, and Ben Johnson.

> *John of the Cross wrote that every quality or virtue the Holy Spirit produces in our souls has three distinguishing trademarks: tranquility, gentleness and strength. In other words, all our actions must be peaceful, gentle and strong. That suggests an immense depth and steadiness, which flows from our small action now being part of the work of the Spirit.*
>
> —Thomas P. Ryan

Introduction

An Invitation to Conversation

Years ago, I asked Walker Percy, winner of the National Book Award, "In one sentence, what is the best way to write?" He answered, "Write as though you are talking with someone."

In these pages, I hope to converse with you, sharing some of what I have learned and experienced on a spiritual odyssey that began a long time ago. This book is an invitation to link your soul with mine, so that together we might explore the ways of the One who would have us think, listen, and love as Christ did and now does—not by imitation, but through a gradual inner transformation.

At the end of each unit, you will find a practice that might help you to move forward on your unique spiritual journey.

May this book evolve into a friend who encourages you to value more deeply your inherent goodness and the privilege of accepting yourself as you are—as did a child in a story told by Jean Vanier, the founder of *L'Arche*, a community that ministers to the mentally challenged.

Vanier recalls meeting a handicapped child at a special Communion service. Afterward, the child's uncle approached his mother and said, "Now wasn't that a beautiful service? The only sad thing about it is that your boy didn't understand a thing."

The child overheard that. With tears in his eyes he told his mother, "But I *did* understand, mom. Don't worry. You know that Jesus loves me *just the way I am.*"

The child knew that it was all right to be other than what his uncle assumed him to be. It was all right to be severely handicapped. It was all right to be raw and fragile. It was all right for Jesus to love him just as he was.

With a deep bow of respect, dear reader, my prayer is that something in these pages might help you to become, from the deepest level of soul, what every member of our species is meant to be: gentleness incarnate, in the image and likeness of God. May you live forever in God.

Of Silence, Kindness, and Prayer

Life is a sacred adventure. When we are born, it lies open to us like a 360-degree vista, waiting to be explored. As we grow up, much of what we encounter conspires to shrink this sacred circle into a tight little system that we call ourselves. As we grow older, this circle tightens and tightens until it seems that we are at the center of a very small world, a kingdom that we control and rule.

—Carlos Warter

CHAPTER 1

The Round Dance of the Trinity

> Lucy looked hard at the garden and saw that it was
> not really a garden at all but a whole world, with its
> own rivers and woods and sea and mountains…
>
> "I see," she said, "this is still Narnia, and more real
> and more beautiful than the Narnia down below…
> I see…world within world, Narnia within Narnia…"
>
> "Yes," said Mr. Tumnus, "like an onion: except that
> as you continue to go in and in, each circle is larger
> than the last."
>
> —C. S. Lewis

And so we begin with a story that you may find hard to believe.
It's about a seven-year-old child and what she did on the eve of
9/11.

Colette, a deeply intuitive woman, wandered into the
recreation room holding a swallowtail butterfly. Her daughter
was leaning forward, staring at a collection of building blocks.

"Katie, look what I found!"

No response. Her stare was locked inside the building
blocks.

"You don't want to see it?"

Katie continued to stare. Intensity pushed to a high level.
You could feel it.

Colette went to the garden to release the butterfly. When she returned, Katie was stacking one block on top of another. Colette's palms started to sweat.

The child shaped a second set of blocks. It stood next to the first.

Then she went to a desk and returned with a paper plane. Moments later she ran it through the first tower. It collapsed. Katie stared at the scattered blocks for several minutes. Then she raised her hand slowly, gripping the paper plane between thumb and finger, and ran it through the second tower.

Colette swallowed hard. It took a while for a barely audible question to break through the silence, "Honey...why did you do that?"

The answer came solemn and slow.

"That's just the way it is, Mama. That's just the way it is."

After the angel of death has led you over a beaten path, past the outer margin of the other world and into the next, what do you suppose you will want to do?

When I was eleven, my friend Sydney and I were lounging on a sandy bank one night, pondering that question. Sydney was lying with hands crossed under his head watching a cloud go by when he said, "I'd like to go lantern fishing and hear the sound of drums, bass, percussion, horns, piano, accordion. I'd like to play the alto sax to *chanky chank*. Of course, I'd have to explain to God that this means Cajun music. Can you imagine him in the back of a pickup truck doing *chanky chank*?"

As for me, I told Sydney that I'd like to have a notebook filled with questions, one of them starting with *How is it possible that...?*

This is what I'll ask God after he hears what happened on the eve of 9/11: *How could it be that Katie was able to see into the future with such accuracy?*

Perhaps he will tell me that her vision emerged from inside Narnia within Narnia—a vast inner land with no beginning in time or edges in space.

⟨⟩

The physicist Deepak Chopra, former chief of staff at New England Memorial Hospital, depicts an immensity vibrating inside our inmost selves. He notes that Western physicists already recognize that a "quantum field" lies at the deepest level of the natural world. A "quantum" is the smallest unit of light, or electricity, or other energy that can exist in our universe.

At close range it becomes clear that the atom is composed of tiny bits of matter spinning around immense empty space. According to Chopra, *this spaciousness rivals the vast regions of intergalactic space*. The interval between two electrons is proportionately wider than the one separating the earth and the sun. But if we look closer at these bits of subatomic matter we might notice that they are not material, and not really solid, even if they give that appearance. They are vibrations of energy that *look* solid.*

We humans might appear to be nothing but concrete matter. But while our bodies may seem to be *only* concrete, they also consist of vibrations of energy whirling deep inside each segment of our humanity.

A universe that rivals the immensity of intergalactic space lives inside Katie, and in everyone. Our inmost depths—home to the image of God—reflect God's immensity, infinitely wider than the interval separating the earth and the sun.

⟨⟩

---

* Deepak Chopra, *Perfect Health: The Complete Mind/Body Guide*, rev. and updated (New York: Three Rivers Press, 2000), 168–69.

Human beings and trees have this in common: each is a marvel of depth within depth, world within world, Narnia within Narnia. On the eve of 9/11, did Katie stare from within the deep silence of that marvel?

◊

Right now, snow is covering the pear tree outside my window. But spring is near. Soon the snow will melt, Narnia will appear, and the pear tree's green will break into the sunlight. Its familiar shape will return—starting at its outer parts, ending in its inner world, its Narnia within Narnia.

If we could "see"—in the biblical sense of "experience"— we would see more than the green branches and pears of this world of Narnia. Our awareness would penetrate layers of depth: molecular, atomic, subatomic....We would attend to these levels as they melted into light, and the silence of infinity: the celestial *no sound* of Narnia within Narnia.

If we could see, we might sink into an intimate depth shared by every pocket of creation: the level where—according to Bell's Theorem—everything is connected.

Physicists are aware that an unknown force, traveling faster than the speed of light, ties everything and everyone together. But to see this force field we would have to tiptoe quietly down "long flights of stairs," to the "level" where music is flowing out of unseen strings. Then we might settle down into the point where Narnia transcends Narnia.

◊

If we were to experience people as they really are, we would enjoy the same pattern of beauty and order found in the tree. At one level, we would contact Narnia: senses, thoughts, and feelings—all at different layers of depth. At another level, we might touch the elbow of a world beyond experience, the spaciousness of all there is: the second Narnia.

If we could see, we might experience the world of the whole person, its parts intersecting like the marvelous upsidedown tree of the *Katha Upanishad* of India—its roots in the heavens. We might experience the totality of Narnia, inner plus outer: the antithesis of choosing one world (either vertical or horizontal) over the other; and sink into the silence of apparently divergent "worlds" intersecting to form the temple of the Great Round Dance.

The ancient Greek Fathers depict the Trinity as a Round Dance: an event that has continued for six thousand years, and six times six thousand, and beyond the time when humans *first* knew time. An infinite current of love streams without ceasing *to and fro, to and fro, to and fro*: gliding from the Father to the Son, and back to the Father, in one timeless happening. This circular current of trinitarian love continues night and day, inside its unique Narnia within Narnia. The orderly and rhythmic process of subatomic particles spinning round and round at immense speed echoes its dynamism.

Lord Jesus, at a time when I did not yet realize that your ways were not my ways, I felt that you could have done something to prevent 9/11. I did not understand.

Then I heard about a survivor of the Holocaust who, in Israel, was looked on with a sneer of disdain: Why did you do nothing to resist the Nazis? Why were you not like the heroic Jews in the Warsaw ghetto?

This added to the survivor's bitterness. She told a friend that when she died, she would put God on trial for remaining a spectator in the death camp.

One morning in Tel Aviv, the survivor had a near-death experience. Her friend waited until she had recuperated to ask, "Did you put him on trial?"

"Yes. I understand."

"And so…?"

"It's beyond language. You'll have to see for yourself."

/\

Lord Jesus, remember when I accused you of doing nothing to prevent 9/11? You kept silent for a long time.

Then you said, "Trust Me."

You drew me into the center of the Great Round Dance. I had no idea that you were doing that. But that is when I began to trust you, but only a little bit.

Now I am at peace, trusting more, doing my best to serve all where you are many…in a way which only you see clearly.

Like the survivor of the Holocaust, I will understand…when the time is right.

CHAPTER 2

The Silence at the Bottom of the Soul

"I love silence," Katriel continued, "but beware:...
some are sterile, malignant. My father can
distinguish between them with ease; I only with
difficulty. There is the silence which preceded
creation; and the one which accompanies the
revelation on Mount Sinai. The first contains chaos
and solitude; the second suggests presence, fervor,
plenitude. I like the second. I like silence to have a
history and be transmitted by it."

—Elie Wiesel

Many have sensed something mysterious and compelling about
a vast body of water. Like an oracle, it links itself to the Lord of
the universe. Its silence speaks of God's intimations in the briny
deep of the human heart.

Did you know that if you drop a piece of metal into ocean
waters, it will take an hour to descend eleven thousand meters
before hitting bottom? Dynamic energy increases at each successive level of water. It swells further the closer you get to the
ocean floor.

Gary, a deep-sea diver, felt this ever-deepening power as he
sank toward the bottom of the Romanche Gap—the third deepest spot in the Atlantic Ocean, nearly five miles deep.

As Gary drew close to the ocean floor, its silence overwhelmed him. A door began to unlock inside his heart. But he didn't have to tell the silence that it was all right to come in. It already had asked, *May I keep opening inside your soul?*

Gary thought, *This is what God must be like.*

He was never the same after that.

○

The Hebrew term *dabar* has been translated as "word." But this rendition misses the point. *Dabar* means "event, dynamic happening."

Gary's experience was *dabar*, a sacred energy that awakened something grand in his inmost soul. His life swept onto a road pulsating with light and energy: a path on which the Divine Image would unfold into likeness, but just gradually, under the sign of silence.

Gary is now Br. Leander, a cloistered monk. I stay in touch with him. He says that the memory of the huge silence at the bottom of the ocean keeps reminding him of what God must be like.

○

It is the custom in some African tribes for persons who have not seen each other for a good while to gather in a hut. They sit facing each other in silence—to utter a word would be to defile the climate of quiet pervading the hut. The silence of one person touches the silence of the other, giving birth to an offspring of oneness. After a long time, language begins to emerge from a shared, sanctified silence.

○

Webster's Dictionary defines *silence* as "the absence of sound or noise." Webster has it right, in that silence is the absence of *something*. Silence is not an object among other objects, nor is God. We may speak *about* silence or God, but this is not the same as living these realities.

A vibrant silence, present within the image of God within us, underlies all activity. It differs from the brooding hush that hovers over a breakfast table after parents have quarreled and all you hear is the clatter of knives and forks.

Nor is it the same as the muteness of persons who remain indifferent to the immense suffering caused by unchallenged social injustice.

Nor is it writer's block!

The notion of silence appears to unsettle—or puzzle—no small number of people of all walks of life.

A social consensus prevalent in our culture proclaims that our identity and value depend on what we accomplish and on what others think of us. Given that so many buy into this illusory construct, something as "unproductive" as silence is not often taken seriously.

The evaluation of silence differs from culture to culture. In the West, if you notice that someone is silent for a prolonged period of time, the tendency might be to ask, "Are you all right?" Or the silence might be interpreted as a sign of unbalanced introversion or isolation or passive aggression.

In India, they would say of the silent one, *Ah muni!* (*Ah, there is a holy soul!*)

The ancients gave a name to the more mature stage of inner silence: *hesychia* (heh-zih-*kay*-a). The power of profound inner quiet increases to the extent that the image of God changes into likeness. That image reflects who he is. And since, among other things, *God is Silence.* . . .

Hesychia is a vast field of energy vibrating at the deepest layer of soul. It is within all human beings. The ancient monastic tradition identifies it as the indispensable condition for loving others in a generous—and genuine—way.

Like the energy that increases at each successive layer of ocean waters, power swells the deeper we drop beneath one meter of inner silence after another. As we sink deeper, all models of time, space, and matter are left behind. As we reach the ground of the soul, its silence is kin to the energy at the bottom of the ocean. At that point, we touch the depth of the image of God.

Inner silence is gentle. As it ripens, less and less thoughts drift through the mind during a serious conversation, less pondering an answer to what is heard. At an advanced stage of inner stillness, one will listen to the other, with only silence inside. Then one will be listening more the way that Christ listened and still listens: with bare attention. No assumptions, no judgments, no preconceived ideas, no projections pasted over experience.

Listening. Just that.

At times it may feel as though nothing is happening in that vast silence. And yet *so much is happening!*

In the endless region of our inner landscape, bit by tiny bit, we are transformed into the likeness of Christ, as we are changed by waves and waves of Silent Mercy; so that gradually we come to speak, think, and love as Christ does: gently, without fuss, in a marvel of beauty.

Not all in the more superficial layers of silence is sacred. At the surface of inner quiet, holiness may share space with sinister intruders. But the saints assure us that at the bottom of the soul, at the level of profound silence, we are most protected from the influence of dark forces.

Only God has access to those regions of depth. They are the home he shares with us.

Interior silence, *relational*?

You may recall this from one of the psalms: "Be still, and know that I am God!" (Ps 46:10). The scriptural term *to know* is a translation of the Hebrew *yadah*, "to connect with someone in an intimate way." For the Jew, *yadah* and sexual intercourse are synonymous.

We connect with God through *yadah*. In the silence of intimacy, we are one with Christ, yet other than him. This means that this kind of silence is not inert, distant, or disinterested. At its heart is a fidelity that takes us seriously.

Three o'clock in the Alps, on a quiet amber night.

Unable to sleep, I recall something that the Jungian analyst Morton Kelsey had said: during the long hours of insomnia, we must listen. What if God wants to communicate an important message?

And so I open the conversation:

Lord Jesus,

What were those bagpipes in the distance which have fallen asleep?

When I experience certain feelings, you assure me that they are angels bearing messages, revealing secrets.

This time around, the angel is grief, drifting toward me, meaning no harm. I slip my hands into my pockets and wait for it to draw closer. When it does, I lean toward it, eager to hear what message—or secret—it is bringing me.

But like you and the silence, it just stands there, gazing into my eyes, making not the slightest sound. For me, the angel is no stranger.

At exactly four, grief disappears.

Where has it gone? Has it fallen deep into one of my pockets? Or made its way into the large body of one of the bucks down by the river? Has it dropped into the quiet open spaces of my soul?

Lord Jesus,

We are alone—immersed in the silence, always the same silence—as still another secret appears, pinching truth with awesome dignity, keeping what it knows to itself…for now.

CHAPTER 3

Rambling at Ease

Reverence without love is an imperfection;
but love without reverence is nothing at all.
—A Jewish saying

Chaim Potok's *The Chosen* depicts a father's painful memories of his early years with his son, Daniel. When the boy reads a book about a suffering Jew, his father is shocked: Daniel is indifferent to his pain; and yet is puffed up with pride over his ability to recount the story from memory.

"He was a mind in a body without a soul," the father laments. "I went away and cried to the Master of the universe, 'What have You done to me? A mind like this I need for a son? A *heart* I need for a son; a *soul* I need for a son; *compassion* I want from my son, righteousness, mercy, strength to suffer and carry pain. *That* is what I want for my son, not a mind without a soul!'"*

Locked in the head, Daniel would be unable to make sense of Narnia within Narnia, nor of the gentle strength of deep faith: the unbroken melody that lives within the silence of the inmost self.

* Chaim Potok, *The Chosen* (New York: Random House, 1987), 283.

It is not enough for a tree to be blessed with leaves, branches, trunk, and shoots. It must have roots.

To be human, it is not enough to feel, think, remember, dream, and imagine. We must have roots; a silence that reaches down into the silence of God, the Origin of faith.

Daniel was living an extremely partial life because he was split off from his roots, as well as from the leaves, branches, and shoots of the human version of the tree—his feelings, his heart, any semblance of compassion.

Daniel had vanished inside a thick wall, appearing only now and then, to listen to the wailing of the wind.

⟨⟩

Our "human roots" blossom in our inmost self, grounded in the One whose "tender root tips" send life to every segment of our humanity.

To allow the outer structure of our lives—body, mind, senses—to be in sync with soul is to integrate boundaries with the boundless.

But Daniel was satisfied only with the boundaries that bound him to his mind.

⟨⟩

When C. S. Lewis says that we long to be on the inside of a door we have always seen from the outside, he may be referring to people who have not had much contact with soul, if at all. *At an unconscious level*, these persons—including Daniel—may be yearning to open a door, at the midpoint between their inner and outer lives: a longing to enliven the permanent side of their humanity—and to welcome, with a grateful heart, the gift of faith.

⟨⟩

I don't remember the year but only the observation. It was made by the Abbot Primate, the monk who oversees Benedictine monasteries throughout the world. After visiting one abbey after another, he told his secretary, "They look so sad. Is it because they are without woman?"

The observation awakened in me the memory of an abbot who seemed sad, too, and lost. He was not gentle.

He loved to talk...*about*. But *experience*? That was for dreamers, for ethereal monks: the ones who, as Thomas Merton had done one afternoon, would take a jeep into the woods and total it.

The abbot enjoyed good liturgy, incense, great intellects, voices on pitch, books and articles on philosophy, and God and community. He loved to gather scholars from inside and outside the monastery to talk *about* such things.

But the abbot seemed half-alive, lost in cobwebs that recognized as real only what is manifest. The man was incapable of relating to the unseen half of our humanity. He held in contempt the one or two "mystics" who "floated around the abbey grounds."

"I'd get rid of them," he said, "but I can't. They're in final vows."

One day he leaned in my direction, to tell me, as though conveying a truth gone undisclosed for centuries, "If you can't see, smell, taste, hear, or touch it, then it just plain *ain't*."

Without realizing it, the abbot may have yearned to be on the inside of a door he had always seen from the outside. But because he was not open to spiritual practices that might lead him past the mind, at a conscious level, he concluded that nothing existed beyond the door.

We are not complete human beings without the outer self through which we ponder, make choices, set fire to our hopes and dreams, make bread and honey, weep—whether in joy or in sorrow—and decide if we would engage in soul work or not.

Through this outer self, we know that the morning star is up, and sense the vastness of God as the sun slides down. Our body offers a deep bow of thanksgiving to the gentleness of the noble heart of Jesus.

Each indispensable facet of our humanity belongs to an outer sphere of life that is always changing, especially the workings of the mind, where thoughts and images are continually arising and passing away.

A new set of atoms is born each month to replace 98 percent of the atoms of our body, and every four weeks, we take on new skin. Events happen, then vanish. Feelings? Memories? The same thing.

Fr. Matthew Kelty recalls that Thomas Merton "was as merry a man as I have known, yet he had a depth of sadness it were best not to mention."

If the changing outer sphere were to determine who we are, then it would follow that on one day Merton's identity would amount to being as merry a man as Fr. Matthew had ever known; while the next morning his identity might be reduced to a mood—"I *am* sad."

◊

One way to interpret anxiety is to look at it as a fear or dread of losing not just a particular value in one's life, but one's existence as a whole. At times, the anxious person misperceives impending danger as jeopardizing *everything*. This happens when he bases his identity on what is outside him: circumstances, the opinions of others, his work…whatever is always changing.

Not so with the one who realizes that he *is*, and that his most profound identity—rooted in Christ at the level of Narnia *within Narnia*—is beyond destruction. The ancient Chinese writer Chuang-tzu would say that such a person is *rambling at ease*, disentangled from—yet honoring and living—what is always in flux.

◊

As death approaches and the need for food and drink diminishes, the mind and the outer side of our humanity starts to edge away. Sometimes the dying person resembles an innocent child: no pretense, no effort to manipulate or control, no clinging to defense or denial, no compulsion to "make it to the top" or play a role.

Perhaps in the long hours of awaiting the angel of death, Daniel—now with deep lines in his face—might at last come to resemble that innocent child.

CHAPTER 4

Contemplation in the Grotto

Often when a person is quite unprepared for such a
thing, and is not even thinking of God, he is
awakened by His Majesty, as though by a rushing
comet or a thunderclap.

—St. John of the Cross

The awakening might happen on a day when you finally realize
that you can't go on alone. So you kneel very still, heart and
mind cloudy, energy scattered. As time passes, you sense that the
One who works in the powerful silence of this sacred space is
starting to move inside you. Threads start to untangle...here, in
the Grotto, at Notre Dame.

At freshman orientation, Fr. Driscoll arches his thin frame
slightly forward—a prelude to an impassioned invitation to visit
the Grotto. "Please go. You don't have to stay long. I'll guarantee
that you will be blessed."

A hand goes up, "What's the Grotto?"

"A replica of a cave in Lourdes, France, where the Madonna
has performed many miracles."

Another hand rises, one of many, "What kind of miracles?"

"The list is long. A paralytic starts to walk. A face disfigured in a fire becomes clear, even radiant. Memories of torture begin to heal. Despair turns into hope."

Fr. Driscoll asks if anyone has heard of Dr. Tom Dooley. A freshman says that he was famous for his humanitarian work in Asia.

"When he was dying of cancer," Fr. Driscoll recalls, "he talked about a gnawing, yearning passion to be at the Grotto. He felt that it was the rock to which his life was anchored."

With his mind and heart experiencing the Grotto from afar, the late Dr. Tom Dooley wonders if the students appreciate what they have, while they have it.

I didn't, until I went there late one fall afternoon, after the birds had quieted down.

Initially, I found nothing special about the Grotto. I knelt like everybody else along a railing, thoughts racing through my head. Then, as my neighbor rose to leave, my mind went silent. An invisible curtain opened and I was drawn into the heart of a strange, incomprehensible experience. Within moments, my tongue felt immobile. Speech was impossible. I was unable to think, imagine, remember, or feel. Without realizing it, the Spirit had suspended these faculties.

(Thomas Merton recalls the day that a trapdoor opened inside him. He fell into stellar space.)

After my faculties were suspended, my own version of the trapdoor flew open. I sank.

When I opened my eyes after twenty minutes, it felt as though I had been "away" for less than a second. I was quiet inside, with no sign of disorientation.

Had I been in a land that is timeless and eternal—old, yet young?

Have you seen birds riding the wind? For the babies, it's not a matter of beating their wings but of learning to lend them to the wind. As I walked slowly to my dorm, I was a bird riding the wind.

I said nothing to my friends about what had happened. The next morning I awoke at ten to six: enough time to go downstairs to sign in. This was the first phase of an unquestioned tradition called "dawn patrol," what the Holy Cross Fathers were convinced was an ingenious solution to the challenge of getting students into the chapel for Mass. We passed it on the way to and from the sign-in desk.

But the strategy didn't work. Almost all of us went back to bed.

I moved past the chapel and went as far as the stairs leading to the second floor. I stopped and leaned against a wall for a while, thinking about nothing in particular. A friend passed by and said, over his shoulder, "What's goin' on?"

I felt a gentle impulse to return to the vicinity of the chapel. A life-like statue of the Madonna stood to the right of the entrance. I gazed into her eyes, and she into mine. After a while, I sensed that it was time to enter the chapel.

I walked in. Without realizing it, I tasted the first moments of what was to be an ever-deepening bond with the Eucharist. After Mass I stood in front of the Madonna again. Our eyes linked. Not knowing why, I whispered, "Thank you."

After a few days of going to the chapel each morning, my friends wanted to know what was going on.

I shrugged my shoulders.

I wanted to tell them, but couldn't get it out.

CHAPTER 5

When Dialogue Disappears

> In contemplation all dialogue, interior or exterior,
> disappears. At this level subject and object have
> been transcended, as have yesterday and tomorrow,
> frustration and euphoria.
> —Willigis Jäger, OSB

In the Catholic era in which I lived, it was understood that to be holy, you had to be a priest. And so after graduation, I entered a seminary.

Since that event in the Grotto, I had not experienced anything like it. But on a Sunday afternoon, alone in a dorm chapel, it happened: the tongue was bound, along with the other faculties. I sank.

After that, this mysterious event appeared from time to time with its usual unpredictability, but without a set format. I did not always sense that the faculties were bound. I would just sink. As at Notre Dame, I kept this to myself.

After three years, I entered a monastery. One morning I was sitting in the scriptorium near a pendulum clock, listening to its gentle sounds—*tick tock, tick tock, tick tock*....I felt quieter and quieter...and started to sink.

When I "returned," a Brother made a sign, "You asleep?"

I nodded, with a faint smile.

The clock sent a message, "It's time to tell someone about those experiences."

I asked to speak with an old monk, the one with the gentle eyes. In his office, Fr. Jacob listened carefully to my tale, nodding occasionally, a faint smile appearing now and then. I detected no look of concern.

When I stopped talking, Fr. Jacob said, rather casually, "That's contemplation."

I had heard the term, but had been told that it was a lofty state reserved for the spiritually mature, or for people who were well on their way to sanctity. But since I was neither, I took no interest in the subject.

Fr. Jacob distinguished between two kinds of contemplation. In the first, you *do something* to prepare for intimacy with our Lord, such as sitting at home or in a church, quietly aware of God's presence. Contemplation of the second kind involves *no activity* from our side. The experience just happens. It is unexpected, an unmerited gift of God.

Fr. Jacob explained that the second kind is called infused contemplation—from the Latin *infundere*, "to pour in." Having suspended the faculties, God pours his grace into the soul. He causes our spirit to sink into what Fr. Jacob said was "a very special place."

Soon it became clear that if we are aware of God, we are experiencing him in a way mediated by the intellect, senses, or imagination, and not directly. Infused contemplation is a state of being. We are one with God. That's all.

◊

Many sincere persons are convinced that when they cease feeling God's presence, he must have wandered off somewhere and forgotten to return. They ponder on it well, and end up feeling abandoned. At this delicate stage of the odyssey, it is essential that someone of depth accompanies them—or that they read a book by a spiritual author, or hear a talk by an authentic mentor.

I wonder if the reason that so many left the Catholic charismatic renewal is because they had equated God's attendance with a feeling of his presence. With leaders for the most part unfamiliar with the purpose of aridity, these persons felt abandoned. Then they moved away from the movement—and perhaps even from prayer. Without guidance, they remained unaware that aridity has the potential to gradually dissolve the notion that God is present only if we feel his presence; and to grasp the truth that we move inside the vastness of our Creator, at every moment. To return to an essential point, contemplation bypasses feelings.

Desolation in prayer helps to make room for the gift of contemplation. It may appear that one is left with empty space. But this space is not hollow; rather it is a lively silence that readies us to receive the gift of infused contemplation, if God is of a mind to bestow it.

A method known as Centering Prayer emphasizes openness to God's action in one's life; a waiting, a wakeful receptivity. It disposes a person to receive the gift of infused contemplation.

Desolation challenges anthropomorphism at its worst: the portrayal of God as dangerous, toxic, remote, and indifferent.

◊

From time to time, I become, once again, the naïve, young freshman who walked into the Grotto and received a *lagniappe*—

Louisiana French for an unexpected surprise; an amazing gift that is neither merited nor deserved, and is certainly no reason to swagger.

And you, dear reader: who knows? Alone under a strong moon, the Spirit might surprise you with that gift.

Knowing what contemplation means, should the tongue feel immobile and you start to sink, you will fare far better than some who received the gift in vain: persons who feared that they were on the brink of annihilation, that they were hallucinating, having an epileptic seizure, or standing at the edge of madness.

It took me years to speak in public about contemplation. After my talk at a retreat, a few thanked me for explaining the experience they had been so afraid to disclose.

Should God grace you with the gift of contemplation, rest assured that the word *lagniappe* will mean, for you, far more than the name of a newspaper in the backwoods of Cajun Louisiana!

CHAPTER 6

The Power of His Name

> The practice of keeping the Name of Jesus ever
> present in the ground of one's being was, for the
> ancient monks, the secret of the "control of
> thoughts," and of victory over temptation. It
> accompanied all the other activities of the monastic
> life, imbuing them with prayer.
>
> —Thomas Merton

The power of his name, in three scenes.

The first. I remember well the day I introduced some college students to the power present in the invocation of the name "Jesus." Some listened closely while others crossed and uncrossed their legs, boredom meandering behind their eyelids.

A few weeks later, when we were deep into winter, two of my more serious students were traveling on a sleek Iowa highway. The driver, Eric, slammed his foot on the brakes, thinking it wise to move slower since a large truck was speeding toward them.

The car spun out of control. It whirled around on the highway. The truck driver slowed down, but it was too late. It was impossible to avoid a collision.

Eric called out, "Jesus, help us!"

The next day, he rushed to my office to tell the story. He was loud. Shifting from one hip to the other, he said, "When I called on *the Name* my car drifted to the side of the road. *I felt that a giant hand had moved it!*"

The second. A man is driving on a bridge. It's winter, and the surface is sleek. A truck is approaching. When the man applies the brakes to slow down, the car spins out of control.

The driver, who belongs to a Mafia family, cries out, "Jesus!"

"It was so strange...so powerful," he tells me. "I don't recall *ever* calling on Jesus for help....The truck driver gaped at me in disbelief....I was shaking from head to toe...."

He tells me this in a low tone, as though afraid that a Mafioso might be eavesdropping, "*It was like a giant hand had taken hold of the car and nudged it to the side.*"

The third. A priest and a nun are driving on an icy highway in New England. The road is slick, even with the sun occasionally sending a few volts on the land below as it begins to descend over the horizon.

At that moment, a large truck approaches them.

Fr. Lafitte says, "I reckon I'd better slow down with that truck coming at us at such a high speed." He bends his long frame as sneakers press on the brakes.

The car spins out of control.

He gasps, "Jesus!"

Fr. Lafitte told me, "*It was as though a giant hand had come out of nowhere and pushed the car off to the side.*"

A shaken nun had trouble getting the words out, "Thank you for doing that."

"For doing what?"

"For calling on Jesus to help us."
"But how would you know that? *I didn't say it out loud!*"

Perhaps you are as much at ease as I am in honoring the names attributed to God in different cultures: *the Great Light, Abba, Yahweh, Allah, the Great Spirit, Ruah, the Friend.*

Then there is *the Great Heart*, which is how Jesus was known in the most ancient days of Christian experience. This name reflects the wonder felt in the presence of the One whose outpouring of kindness and compassion was so limitless, so considerate, so gentle.

But also there is the *Shekhinah.*

Speaking out of the ancient Jewish tradition, Elie Wiesel writes, "Happy is he who unites his words and his silence with the words and silences of the *Shekhinah*, the Divine Presence which prowls about this place. Soon, brothers, you will feel its breath. Let me be the one to announce this to you….At midnight you will hear the *Shekhinah*."*

Have you heard of Kabir? He was a poet who lived in India during the fifteenth century. He called God the *Secret One.* Kabir's intense life of devotion to the Lord of the universe flowed with a continuous—and mutual—love energy. "As the river gives itself into the ocean," Kabir wrote, "what is inside me moves inside You."

The poems of Jalal al-Din Rumi are ecstatic, describing how it feels to slowly evolve in the company of the One he called *The Friend.*

---

* Elie Wiesel, *A Beggar in Jerusalem* (New York: Schocken, 1997), 81.

But we have also been blessed with a lesser-known, poetic name of God: *The Great Blue Heron*, who speaks to me in the poem "God's Grandeur" by Gerard Manley Hopkins:

The Holy Ghost over the bent
World broods with warm breast
and with ah! bright wings.

Without the fidelity of The Great Blue Heron, I would wander around aimlessly, hands in my pockets. But with him, I move forward with purpose. The Heron gives himself to me with gentle intensity, like a man who will never see his wife again, or Christ at the Last Supper.

Here is a mini-exorcism prayer: *In the name of Jesus Christ, may Satan, demons, and spirits leave me.* (To say, "In the name of Jesus," is essential. *The name* must accompany *the prayer.*)

The road through the land of likeness can be unpredictable, even treacherous. At a time you least expect, you may need this prayer.

CHAPTER 7

The Second Heart

In our youth, we don't realize how important a
spiritual practice is; when middle-aged, we claim to
be too busy to practice; and when we are old, it's
too late.

—A saying of the Kagyu tribe in Kenya

Some feel that the sixties and seventies were the most important
era in American history—a time when persons of all ages and
backgrounds became aware of viable options. You could travel
the path of social justice or the charismatic renewal or the civil
rights movement. It was all right to belong to a twelve-step
group or to be in therapy. More accepted their bodies and sexu-
ality as sacred aspects of their humanity. The graces of the
Second Vatican Council abounded, and along with it, ecu-
menism.

A significant option was the choice to travel the path of
deep inner prayer or meditation of the Eastern kind.

Many passed through doors held open by spiritual mentors.
One of these, a woman in her early twenties, approached a teacher
self-consciously. She asked, "Will you teach me to meditate?"

A young man waiting in another room told a student that
he was looking for new worlds. He seemed guarded—as though
standing from behind an invisible black iron fence. When it was

his turn to see the spiritual teacher, he requested help "to go deep in prayer."

The spiritual master taught them—with gentleness and explicit instructions.

"Blessings upon you," he said, after an hour with each.

A great strength arose and passed into the hearts and souls of these two seekers. But after a period of time, they grew weary of what they had learned and stopped practicing.

The teacher, Chogyam Trungpa, was aware of a growing pattern: youth learning to pray or meditate, then practicing for a while, then stopping. Apparently exasperated, one day he told an audience, "*It's one insult after another.* If from the start you are not serious about your practice of meditation, if there is ambivalence, I would advise you not to start. But if you have begun, please do finish."

Insult after insult does not mean abuse or humiliation, but hardships and challenges that open into opportunities for inner evolution.

It is said that one night Rabbi Akiva was lost in a shipwreck in the middle of a sea. Only he survived. When somebody asked how he did it, Akiva answered, "Whenever a wave arose, I bent into it."

To bend into the wave is to take seriously what, in the twelfth-century, St. Bernard called *alternation of experience*: whatever occurs—whether it be pleasant, unpleasant, or neutral—is an opportunity for the unfolding of the image of God into likeness.

Another way to understand this model is to appeal to the paschal mystery, with each day corresponding to an aspect of alternation: Good Friday—unpleasant; Holy Saturday—neutral; and Easter Sunday—pleasant.

To exclude Good Friday would be to talk about something other than this mystery.

We are aware from daily living that we are bound to experience peace and joy, as well as disillusion, illness, confusion.... By accepting alternation, we stay realistic about what our life is and is not; and remain stable and connected with truth. Why turn away from any aspect of alternation? Everything is a means to transformation, even of the slightest kind.

The spiritual teacher Pema Chödrön bent into a wave when she looked straight into the eyes of a traumatic situation in which—as she puts it—her whole reality gave out on her. For Pema, it was the "Good Friday" side of alternation of experience. It happened when her husband told her that he was having an affair and wanted a divorce.

Pema remembered the sky and its immensity, and the sound of the river and the steam rising up from her tea. It was a timeless moment in which not a single thought crossed her mind. She recalls nothing—just the light and a deep, unbounded stillness. Then she regrouped, picked up a stone, and threw it at her husband.

Pema Chödrön's "Good Friday" led her into a new depth of freedom. When the marriage fell apart, she struggled to return to some kind of comfort, to a safe harbor. In the end, she became keenly aware that the deconstruction of her clinging self was the only way to go.

Years ago when I applied for admission to the monastery, a monk wondered, "Why would you ever want to come here? You have it made out there."

I told him that I wanted to be stretched.

"*Stretched?*"

I said that "in the world" I *did* have it made. I enjoyed a good social life, was blessed with a remarkable group of friends, lived in an artist colony of seven thousand citizens and fifteen art galleries, and maintained an enriching relationship with the Benedictine monks who lived on the outskirts of town. I was a teacher of a type of meditation unique to the Vedic culture of India, which predated Hinduism. I had written a book and was working on another.

But I had been able do anything I wanted, when I wanted. Now I yearned to be stretched by living alternation of experience, which in its "Good Friday" aspect would require me *not* to do anything I wanted, when I wanted.

I followed an inner impulse, born of the Spirit of Jesus, which led me to continue my odyssey as a member of an imperfect monastic community: the kind that did its best to live a balanced life of prayer, work, silence, solitude, kindness, and gentleness.

And yet I didn't realize the extent of the *insults* that awaited me, as one year drifted into another.

Long before I entered the monastery, I joined almost two hundred other young people for a six-month program of meditation on an island off the coast of Spain. The sessions lasted most of the day.

The routine was stark, demanding: solitary hours of meditation in our rooms. Between each meditation, we breathed through alternate nostrils for five minutes and did yoga for ten. Two minutes of alternate nostril breathing followed, then meditation that lasted an hour.

On the first evening on the island, we gathered for our first meeting with our *guru*, Devindra. Before his arrival, we watched a quiet-faced young Indian woman glide toward the podium in her sari, like someone walking through a dream. Vidyapati offered advice.

"Please do not visit the nearby café for coffee or meat."

A girl with hair in a black knot atop her head raised her hand.

"Why no coffee or meat?"

"Both hinder the process in which you will be engaged."

"What do you mean?"

"Food consists of one of three qualities: *sattva*, *tamas*, and *rajas*. *Sattva* is gentle, peaceful, tender, quiet, energetic. *Rajas* is restless. *Tamas* is dull, heavy, lifeless. You must understand that food has an impact on us in an emotional, physical, and spiritual way. You also find these qualities in a person. If *rajas* predominates, someone is likely to be restless or agitated a good bit of the time…"

Just then Devindra entered the hall. Vidyapati folded her hands in *Namaste*, directing them toward our teacher. So did we—although most had not the slightest idea of what the gesture meant: in essence, *I honor the divine in you.*

Devindra offered his *Namaste* to us. Then he introduced us to reality.

"I'm here to help you to gradually reach the point where you will no longer need me."

A collective groan went up from the audience. Whether consciously or unconsciously, the mindset was, "You are at a high level of consciousness, and I am not. So please think for me."

In time, Devindra made it clear that everyone was expected to think for themselves: "This is not a cult, where the charismatic leader insists that everyone turn over their minds to him."

They failed to understand the role of an authentic *guru*—a term derived from two Sanskrit words: *gu*, "darkness;" and *ru*, "light." The genuine *guru* facilitates—but does not cause—the gradual shift from the darkness of inner slumber to an awakening to, and unfolding of, the divine light radiating inside each of us. The disciple is encouraged to cooperate with the *guru* in this process.

"Don't expect to enjoy wave after wave of bliss," Devindra said. "Of course at times you will enjoy the peace of meditation."

This startled the girl next to me. She turned, almost in desperation, and whispered, "What does he mean, *at times*? Just *at times*?"

She and a number of others had arrived expecting to *at all times* be settled in an interior heavenly abode, wrapped in perpetual bliss. But from that first day, it became clear that we were in for inner purification *to the extreme*, in ways that most of us had never experienced.

It didn't take long for me to feel the truth of what Devindra told us at that first meeting: "This won't be easy. The more you meditate, the more you will be in touch with whatever hinders your evolution. In this gradual knowing, some of you—if not most—will touch unhealed wounds, and you will wish you had never come to the island. But you can't escape this radical self-knowledge; at least, not here."

After a few months, I told one of the old monks from India that I didn't think meditation was helping me: "I've been very outgoing all my life, but here I'm feeling increasingly disconnected."

"This sense of separation will gradually wane," he assured me. "It is part of the process of purification from the many sense impressions and influences of egocentricity, engraved in your unconscious. This doesn't mean that you were *never* selfless! You were, and are, that—*but only* at times and in certain circumstances, and then just *to a certain extent*. I would think that in the past, you tended—at least more often than not—to *appear* kind and loving. *Why?* To be recognized as a virtuous man! But now you are inching toward an authentic generosity, carried out on a more consistent basis—*independent* of the gazes of approval from others, *or even from God*."

In Christian terms, what he meant was that now, as in ancient times, Jesus takes us seriously. He is not there to *approve* of us, but to *affirm* the inherent goodness that we are, as images of his own goodness.

$\lozenge$

A friend who had spent six months meditating on the island said that, toward the end of the last month, he told himself, "*I just want to get out of here in one piece!*"

But after it was "all over," he realized that, by his fidelity to the process, he had ripened beyond the level of consciousness he had brought to the island. *But at the price of so many insults!*

$\lozenge$

Repeated practice of meditation results in a life lived increasingly more from the permanent level of our inmost self.

"This," Devindra assured us, "involves a gradual process of inner stabilization." He likened part of the inner work to the ancient Indian practice of dying a cloth.

"First you dip the cloth in a vat of—let's say—yellow dye," he said. "Then expose it to the rays of the sun. By evening, a tiny fraction of the color will have remained in the cloth. You follow the same procedure each day until the cloth is color-fast."

Devindra explained that in meditation we return to the inmost self repeatedly, each time more rooted in "the place where God is," at the bottom of the soul.

"With each meditation, interior silence deepens," Devindra said. "The silence gained is never lost, even if one were to stop meditating." He emphasized that with dedication to the process, an abiding sense of union with God would grow steadily, and continue to unfold—provided that this is what we wanted.

Many didn't want it. After one or more years of meditation in cities and villages, they stopped meditating: the pattern of which Chogyam Trungpa had been so painfully aware.

Some found the program too much to handle. "I had no idea that Westerners carried so many traumatic memories, so many wounds," Devindra said.

Years later a spiritual master from Thailand came to the same conclusion. While visiting a Buddhist center in America, which practiced a form of meditation different from ours, he spoke with many of the young people who were taking part in an advanced program. The visiting master called the director of the center aside and said, "These youngsters are too raw and fragile to undertake the purification that accompanies meditation. Let them enter therapy, then come back when they have reached at least a modicum of stability. One may grow in consciousness and still remain emotionally immature. It is essential too for everyone to do what it takes to evolve in *all* phases of our humanity."

◊

After our stay on the island, a remnant of the original group moved to the mountains of Switzerland, where we engaged in the same process for six more months. But by now we were accustomed to the incessant intrusion in our lives of *one insult after another*.

◊

That year of meditation helped me to better internalize the primary "slogan" of the desert mothers and fathers of the fourth century—the first Christian nuns and monks: *redite ad cor*, "return to the heart." In Scripture, *the heart* means "the inner self."

We are blessed with two levels of the heart. In the first, a reeducation of love takes place, like the rubbing of sacred oil onto wounds, some of them quite deep. At this layer, resistance to change may begin to unwind.

When Christ warns that all in the heart is not good, he means the first level of the heart. Only he has access to the second layer, at the deepest point of soul, which at its furthest edge opens into infinity.

◊

It's a thick night and I cannot sleep. My mind and senses gather around a fragment of the poem, "Song of the Race," by Pima:

Who is this man running with me,
The shadow of whose hands I see?

I speak into the shadows:

Lord Jesus, you are the Man running with me—not far in the west, around the black mountain, but *here*.

As I move forward, breathing with your Spirit's breath, I realize that I don't know exactly how my journey will unfold in the future.

But you do.

What a blessing to know that you will always be united with me deep within—faithful, even if I am unfaithful!

But this unshakeable fidelity of yours, *no matter what*— doesn't that go against the logic of many in our culture, as it did in yours?

You nod.

I feel the sadness in your voice when you say, "I'm aware of that. But this is how it is."

My Lord Jesus, I'm confident that you believe me when I say that I will do all I can, with your grace, to remain faithful. I would gamble everything to stay awake inside your kindness, and to stand solid within its silent knowing, yearning to hear the secrets you have been waiting to share with me.

CHAPTER 8

Praying with Gentle Strength

Nothing is so strong as gentleness, and nothing so
gentle as strength.

—St. Francis de Sales

How might our nonvocal prayer become more gentle and
strong?

One way is to lower the volume of our interior speech, to
"gentle" it, so that it might more clearly express intimacy with
God.

Our prayer becomes more intimate when the volume of
our speech becomes as gentle as the breath of a musician breathing into a flute.

Listen to Kabir, in one of his poems:

I don't know what sort of a God we have been talking
about.
The caller calls in a loud voice to the Holy One at dusk.
Why? Surely the Holy One is not deaf.
He hears the delicate anklets that ring on the feet of an
insect as it walks.*

* *The Kabir Book: Forty-Four of the Ecstatic Poems of Kabir*, trans. by Robert Bly (Boston:
Beacon Press, 1993), 2.

Gandhi was overheard to say, "There is more to life than speeding it up."

Our breath is eager to help us to slow down so that we might commune with God with greater gentleness.

It is good to introduce the breath into our practice, but usually not until we have grown accustomed to soft and gentle interior speech.

It took some saints a long time to pray the Our Father.

On the inhalation, we say internally, slowly and softly: *Our Father, in heaven...*

Then, exhaling: *...hallowed be your Name...*

Inhaling: *Your kingdom come...*

Continuing in this way to the end.

This approach to nonvocal prayer may help us to grow further into the likeness of the One who said, "Bring me your burdens, for *I am gentle and humble of heart.*

So I bring a burden to him. He extends a hand, palm up. "Please give it to me." Jesus takes the burden and casts it away, like a bucket dropped into the sea.

CHAPTER 9

The Beggar's Final Words

Sometimes a person needs a story more than food to
stay alive.

—Barry Lopez

Night is rising above Calcutta, casting a shadow over a half-
conscious beggar lying on a mat, on eroded soil. Sounds of
agony keep floating toward him: cows lowing in the distance,
afflicted by unmilked udders. They are reaching out to the beggar, joining his suffering with theirs.

The beggar's guard falls when he first meets the thin, angu-
lar nun who is kneeling at his side, wiping the sweat from his
forehead. She knows that his soul is sliding slowly toward the
outer margin of the other world.

She is an Albanian who came to India a long time ago and
never left, a saint whose inner light keeps soaring through the
semidarkness, like the love songs of gypsies in Granada.

She is kindness incarnate.

The beggar's hand is shaking as he gestures to the nun to
draw closer. She leans forward. It takes him a long time to whisper something in her ear, *"I have lived...like an animal....Now I
will die...like an angel."*

The beggar's final words.

The nun kneels in prayer for a few minutes and then folds her hands in the direction of her departed friend: a gesture of *Namaste*.

In India, *Namaste* means "I honor the sacred energy within you, without which the moon would be a dusty hollow and the sun would never wake."

Namaste means "I revere the sacred spaciousness within you, the home of all that lives"—the Assyrian hound howling in one of Lorca's poems, the silence of the stars, the depths of every sea, the rabbi whose cry in prayer is only a whisper.

When Gandhi was murdered, he joined his hands in a gesture of forgiveness, offering *Namaste* to his assassin as he collapsed to the ground.

His final word was *Ram*, "God."

The next morning the Albanian nun goes outside to investigate the sound of a metallic rattle. As she leaves the building, her eyes widen when she notices a young boy, a leper she has not seen for a long time. She runs to the child, stands in front of him with a smile, and with hands folded in front of her heart utters her deeply felt *Namaste*.

The boy answers *Namaste*. The greeting arises from the furthest edge of soul. But he is too young to notice the *Namaste* of the Great Heart: the invisible gesture of the Christ who passes through the inner doors of the poor and the afflicted, with the hem of his rag-garment.

The Prayer of Gratitude

"Father, what name do you give God?" the abbot asked.

"God does not have a name," the dervish replied. "He is too big to fit inside names. A name is a prison. God is free."

The dervish bowed his head and thought. Finally, he parted his lips, "Ah!—that is what I will call Him. Not Allah, but Ah!"

This troubled the abbot. "He's right," he murmured.

—Source unknown

There's a story from the tradition of India in which the lord of rain becomes jealous because Krishna has invaded his territory. He is furious—the townspeople are paying too much attention to Krishna! So he sends down mighty showers to cause the river to rise and drown the townspeople. But Krishna picks up a mountain to stop the rain from coming.

When the townspeople see this, they feel sorry for Krishna: "How can we let him bear so great a burden alone?" They decide to help him by putting sticks against the mountain to give it support.

One of the values of the Prayer of Gratitude might simply be to help a person to "remove his stick," and allow God to hold up the mountain by himself.

Years ago, on that island off the coast of Spain, our guru offered this counsel: "Do less and accomplish more; do least, and accomplish most; do nothing, and accomplish everything."

Not in a passive way, but in a state of inner wakefulness.

It may seem too obvious to say it, but it bears repeating. When Jesus makes a point, it is to be taken seriously.

Only one of the lepers came back to thank me.

Surely, Jesus did not say that to express resentment over the ingratitude of the lepers. Rather, he was punctuating an essential teaching: *Beware of a sense of entitlement.*

Fr. Thomas Keating explains that we don't thank God for *what* happens, but for what *happens*. We don't thank Jesus for a child's death in an accident. Rather, *in some grace-filled way*, the persons who are *capable* of it, or ready for it, might thank God for what his transformative power will bring about in a heart ripped open by grief.

The Prayer of Gratitude—*prayed on the inside, and not aloud*—is about recognizing that each breath is a gift from God. We respond by returning this breath to God, as our own gift to him.

Mind and body go hand in hand. If the mind thinks pleasant thoughts, then the body will feel at ease. But if the body is fidgeting, thoughts will increase.

Before beginning our prayer, we let go into stillness of the body, which stabilizes the mind. We tense the body three times, by clenching the teeth and making a tight fist. Exaggerating tension diminishes tension.

The back is held relaxed and lightly upright. The neck, head, and spine are in a straight line as we close our eyes gently and scan the body from top to bottom. If any area feels tense, we breathe into it. On the exhalation, the tension is released.

The jaw is relaxed, the teeth slightly apart, the tip of the tongue resting lightly on the roof of the mouth. If our attention strays into a thought or series of thoughts, or if we become preoccupied with a feeling, we gently return to the prayer.

A slight "Mona Lisa" smile helps to relax the eyes and muscles of the face. If the shoulders are raised, we allow them to fall.

When we inhale, the abdomen expands as the rib cage rises; when we exhale, the abdomen contracts and the rib cage returns to its original position.

We pause for one or two seconds after inhaling. This is a moment of *stillness*. We pause again after the exhalation, for just a bit longer.

To begin this practice, we let our attention focus lightly at the tip of the nostrils, in anticipation of an incoming breath—our Creator's gift to us.

Exhaling, very softly we utter *Ah*—in almost a whisper. This sound symbolizes the direction toward which we are moving. We sink—in and with Christ—into God's silence, strength, and gentle kindness, at the inmost level of soul.

Ah is by far one of the most powerful sounds in creation. We read in the ancient Vedas, which predate Hinduism, that *Ah* is the first sound uttered by the Creator. Hospice workers utter internally, not aloud, so as to link the rhythm of their breath with the patient's inhalation and exhalation: in, *ah*; out, *ah*....They do this to send encouragement and strength to the patient.

After emerging from a coma, often the patient will ask the hospice worker, "What was that *ah* thing you were doing?" The question is put forth in a tone of voice that expresses appreciation for the kind and generous support offered by the hospice worker.

And so we return to the dervish, who refused to do the equivalent of describing God's face: "A name is a prison. But God is free."

Then he changes his mind, "*Ah*—that is what I will call him! Not Allah, but *Ah*!"

The Prayer of Gratitude resembles the act of diving. Having taken the correct angle, the force of gravity carries us into the water.

In this process, when we exhale—and our breath sinks—the power of the Spirit draws us deep into the vastness of God, who takes in all of creation through our eyes.

We continue in the same way: receiving the gift of breath, returning it as our own gift to God; receiving, then returning; inhaling a sacred breath, exhaling a sacred breath; accepting from the Source, giving back to the Source....

On and on it goes, as we blend into the Great Round Dance.

Breathing in starts from God, and breathing out ends in God.

Breathing in, we are aware that we are inhaling God's gift of breath.

Breathing out, we are aware that we are returning this breath, as our own gift, to God.

This practice may be done for a minute or two, or for ten, or for the recommended twenty.

When we end our prayer, we keep the eyes closed for two minutes and listen to our thoughts.

The Tears
of an
Innocent God

The scandal Jesus caused in that society by mixing socially with sinners can hardly be imagined by most people in the modern world today. It meant he accepted them and approved of them and that he actually wanted to be "a friend of tax collectors and sinners." The effect upon the poor and the oppressed themselves was miraculous.

—Fr. Albert Nolan

CHAPTER 1

The Radiant Christ

"He is not like other sons, Mary," the rabbi boldly
replied.
  "Sometimes when he is alone during the night
and thinks no one is watching him, the whole
circumference of his face gleams in the darkness."
                                    —Nikos Kazantzakis

The great stars that paced back and forth all night over the hut of
an anchorite are gone. In a fraction of a second, our Risen Lord
will awaken the hermit who has overslept, whose dreams have
been the dreams of a Friend praying with and through him during the night. The old man will arise and fall to his knees before a
cross, its center gleaming with light. A sentence will float up from
inside his world within world, his Narnia within Narnia: "Open
my lips, Lord, and my tongue will sing your praise."

Light is striking chords outside his window in the silence
where dawn is breaking and an orphaned fawn is wandering
across an open field, hungry and bewildered, looking for a
mother she will never find.

The sound of swirling eddies nearby welcome me to the
waking state of consciousness. I listen to the silence of the Lamb
whose face sparkles like jasper and carnelian; his right hand is

holding the radiance of seven stars. I bow down to Christ, whose energy is encircled by an emerald-colored rainbow—the Great Heart, whose loving-kindness throws off sparks of light.

Christ's humanity and divinity are stitched together, inseparable, like the two poles of the earth. He is enjoying the "play" that St. Gregory Nazianzen depicts in his poetry, where Luminous Fingers stir the cosmos back and forth, round and round, into forms of every kind. The play of the Risen Christ is a fragrance that never sleeps.

Christ is the God of the Apocalypse: the Alpha and the Omega, the Beginning and the End; as well as a man, whose humanity began as a tiny light in a barn, surrounded by wise men heavy with sleep.

Let's return to Jesus, during his sojourn. He is doing all he can to alert his listeners to the presence of the hard-self corners inside them.

Christ's gaze pierces the insides of the Romans, each one squatting over broken glass—the wreckage of their inner lives. Many have collapsed into spiritual oblivion and emotional stupor. By day, their mouths squeeze into thin lines; by night, they are captive to fitful dreams filled with hanging sentences, broken phrases, and soundless screams.

Christ knows all this, which is why—right in the middle of his passion—he stands absolutely still and asks his Father to forgive the unaware *"for they do not know what they are doing"* (Luke 23:34).

Years after his birth, Jesus becomes the Servant of all. His silence blossoms into unpredictable shades of emotion: appropriate gestures of a deeply feeling person. Christ's life has two sides, one as real as the other. As the Risen Christ, he pervades the universe; as a human being, he is a thinker, whose love is incarnate, a servant, whose silence blossoms into gestures of authentic emotion: a smile, laughter, tears, a lullaby to a sleeping child....

The experience of other cultures offers the same truth of balance and wholeness. Buddha's smile expresses the joy of a man whose breath continually glides in and out of a deep wellspring of silence; the contentment of a human being whose every gesture is unrestricted, unconditional compassion.

Krishna's flute playing marks the intensification of the same joy. His music is human emotion elevated to the highest level, an intensity sweeping out of an ecstatic kernel of light.

The gestures of Buddha and Krishna merge into a third gesture, which focuses on another flavor of human feeling: *the tears of Christ.*

An ancient legend has it that, one day, God entrusted one of his prophets with a mission, "Go quickly and awaken the Fathers of My people: Abraham, Moses....Hurry, Jeremiah! I want to see them, *because they know how to weep.*"

It is true that some may cry for sentimental reasons, or from frustration or hysteria. But tears may signal a breakthrough to an intensity with origins far beneath the surface of things, an experience beyond the reach of "ordinary" feelings. And so it happens that someone might weep at important stages of a given journey: a birth, a death, a wedding, the first stage of conversion....

Jesus weeps over Jerusalem, and over the death of his friend Lazarus. His tears express the same intensity with which he heals the paralytic, washes the feet of his pupils, and returns the boy of Nain to his widowed mother.

Christ's tears reach through miles and miles of light to tell us how much he loves us madly, beyond all rules, conventions, and logic.

The Jewish *Midrash* says that when God sees a child suffer, he drops two tears into the ocean. When they hit the water, the sound is so powerful that you can hear it all around the world.

When the Jewish tradition says that God feels pain, it is quick to add the word *kivyachol*. God feels pain, *kivyachol*. And weeps, *kivyachol*.

When we say of God, *kivyachol*, we mean that he does something in a way we cannot understand. And never will. To grasp it, we would have to be God.

Elie Wiesel was one of the children the Americans liberated from a Nazi death camp. He recalls having a sense of God weeping uncontrollably with and in the Americans.

Kivyachol.

CHAPTER 2

The Tears of an Innocent God

"Why are you crying, Mother? Because the house is burning?"—"It's not the house, son. If I cry it is because a precious document is being destroyed before our eyes."—"What document?" —"Our family tree; it is illustrious, you know."

—Elie Wiesel

A poem by Uri Zvi-Grinberg, paraphrased by Elie Wiesel, is set in World War II in an antisemitic town in Eastern Europe. It has been occupied by a departing SS unit that has killed all the Jews. Deeply moved by Wiesel's paraphrase, I feel compelled to write some lines about it.

I begin by constructing a scene in which an old man is walking slowly through a crowd in the town square. His eyes are fixed on the pavement as though he were staring at eyes trying to send him an unintelligible message. He is Jozef, a retired Protestant minister.

Around three in the afternoon, a stranger appears in the square. When the old man notices him, he thinks, "I sense that this man is so powerful that, if he wanted to, he could shift facets of creation in every direction."

Is that the message he has failed to decode?

The stranger is Jesus. He says, "I have been looking for my people. Would you help me?"

"If I can."

"Where are they?"

"Where are *who*?

"The Jews."

The old man feels an urge to tip his hat, to excuse himself, to walk away.

A few seconds pass by. Jesus repeats, *"Where are the Jews?"* Silence.

"Then," Jesus says, "at least please tell me where I might find their homes."

"If you are looking for your people, there is no point in looking for their homes. I will tell you at last: *they are gone*. After the Jews left, the vultures of various neighborhoods fought each other trying to gain possession of their houses. A priest won, claiming the largest and most prestigious house as his own. He turned it into a rectory. He justified his act by saying that the Jews were being punished because they bore the guilt of their ancestors, who had killed Jesus."

Christ's heart begins to pound.

"You say that this happened after the Jews were gone. *Where did they go?*"

The old man stares at the ground. His lips do not move.

Intuiting the next question, Jozef looks up quickly and holds Jesus' hand tight.

"What about the children? *Where did the children go?*"

His shoulders slumping, Jozef drops his eyes and says nothing. His mouth begins to twitch. After a minute, he answers haltingly, his voice trembling, "The children were called into the main square and told they were going to a picnic with ice cream and games. The boys and girls followed the SS singing and laughing. They stopped two miles from here."

One of the children asked, "Is this where the picnic is?" An officer nodded, "We have a big surprise for you. Look."

His hands shaking, the old man's body seems to be pulling

in every direction as he goes on, "The officer pointed to a big, hollowed out space. The children didn't know that it was going to be a mass grave."

Smiling, the officer said, "Angels live down there! If all of you kneel all along the edges, they will appear!"

When the children knelt, a machine gun finished them off. They tumbled into the grave.

When Jesus hears this, he begins to sob, uncontrollably. Eyes swing in his direction.

"Look! A Jew! How did the SS miss him?"

Unkempt men rush forward to kill Jesus. Within seconds, invisible, he floats through their midst.

Hours later, as he draws close to the resting place of his beloved Jews, Jesus catches sight of an old, emaciated woman standing nearby. Wrapped in a black shawl, her glassy eyes are staring at the mass grave, now covered with earth. When she senses that Someone is walking toward her from behind, she dematerializes.

Jesus breaks down and begins to sob—once again, uncontrollably.

After a while the tears cease. His lips start to move, but you hear nothing. Who is he talking to? Or is he talking to himself, as did a shell-shocked teenaged German soldier whose arm had been blown off at Stalingrad?

When darkness starts to lower itself toward the earth, the moaning of a sudden wind gives rise to an eerie silence. When Christ starts to weep again, the old woman with the glassy eyes reappears. With gentle tenderness, she wipes his tears with her black shawl.

"I understand," she says, in a half-whisper. "I know how it is."

"Thank you."

Jesus walks slowly away, leaving behind the tears of an innocent God.

CHAPTER 3

When God's Ways Seem Irrational

When your life is governed by reason and the
reasonable, beyond a certain point you lose your
touch with God....You no longer speak his
language. When he speaks you do not hear him.
When he acts you do not comprehend....God has
his own way of doing things. To the poor human
mind these ways seem fantastic and...beyond
comprehension.

—Fr. Matthew Kelty

At a time when Tibet was no longer Tibet but a land folded by
strangers, the Chinese imprisoned Patrul, a monk of wrinkled
skin and bent back.

When he first appears in the prison, the old man is shoved
into "the box": a cell carefully crafted, with the ceiling so low that
the prisoner cannot stand; and the walls so spaced that it is impossible to stretch out. After a week, a guard drags a semiconscious
Patrul into a windowless cell. Fifteen years of unspeakable brutal-
ity and isolation end when a guard appears in the humid silence
of his cell and announces that he has been released. Somehow
Patrul gathers the strength to travel to the large Tibetan settlement
in India.

The Dalai Lama puts a gentle hand on his shoulder and

says, "Tell me, Patrul. Was there ever a time when you felt in serious danger?"

"Only when I sensed the possibility of losing the compassion I felt toward my captors—one in particular. The loss of compassion would have split my heart in two."

The Dalai Lama understands. When asked if he hates the Chinese, his answer is always the same, "Why would I want to drag more hatred into the world?"

○

These monks had decided to reject the alternative of remaining folded, as though locked up inside a suffocating interior "box."

Instead, they chose to expand, to unfold; to be faithful to the life purpose held in common by all human beings: to be blended into God or, to paraphrase St. John Damascene, *to be assimilated into God.*

Notice almost the same wording from these men—one from the East, the other from the West—pointing to the same goal: to enliven within themselves the Vast Expanse whose name is Compassion; or as St. John of the Cross would have it, "The Living Flame of Love."

○

The Tibetans were unique manifestations of the love depicted in the Song of Songs; a Kindness that is "strong as death." *Its tongues are flames, a fierce and holy breath. Endless seas and floods, torrents and rivers can never put out the fire of this Gracious Mercy.*

However, in the eyes of countless people in various cultures, the kindness of the monks was irrational, senseless, and unreasonable: *Not to hate the Chinese, who had maimed, tortured and killed so many in Tibet? Not to hate the men who, for years, had brutalized a wrinkled, saintly monk?*

Christ's paradigm of radical equality and inclusivity emphasized a brand of kindness and compassion unknown in Jesus' time.

By his culture's standards, Christ's ways were thought to be incomprehensible: befriending women, lepers, the disabled, the blind, the deaf, the dumb, the equivalent of street people—all forced to beg, since they were deemed unworthy to hold jobs.

Then there were the sinners, branded by anyone "of good breeding and elegant manners" as animals laden with malice—"smelly bums." Jesus felt the inner and outer torments of the outcasts, who went about taut and tight, feeling hopeless—their burdens so unbearable as to suggest suicide as an attractive option.

Jesus must have shocked the disciples, raw and tawdry as they were, by saying that they would do well to become as little children. At the time, children were considered to be subhuman, even commodities, until they reached adulthood.

Wilfrid Harrington, a famous scripture scholar, offers an example of what "the decent people" of Christ's culture thought to be irrational behavior. Harrington did not seem at all startled by a question put to him: "After fifty years of studying, praying, and living the Gospels, would you tell us in a single sentence what has impacted you the most in those texts?"

"The scene in which Jesus invites a tax collector and a prostitute to his feast—*without demanding that they change.*"

According to the theologian Dwight Callahan, Christ's bond with women and "other undesirables" embarrassed his male disciples. "After Christ's ascension," he said, "they had a lot of 'PR' work to do!"

No matter how many times we may have pondered and prayed the parable of the prodigal son, it is worth returning to it at least from time to time. It is a portrait of "unreasonable kindness."

A young man who had drifted off to an alien land now wants to go home—he is out of money and has had enough of degrading living conditions. Unrepentant, his motive for returning is narcissistic. And yet the father not only welcomes him back, but also restores him to full status in the family.

The elder son's furious reaction reflects the logic of the culture: it is irrational to take back someone who is returning for the wrong reasons!

Rembrandt's remarkable painting accentuates the illogic of a love that is divine. The father's face radiates infinite tenderness and compassion as he embraces his son—still unrepentant, still folded inside himself, still dissolving, like melting silver.

A rabbi goes to Elijah, the prophet, with a question, "How long do we have to wait until the Messiah comes?"

Without looking up from his weaving, Elijah reports, casually, that the Messiah has already come.

The rabbi is shocked. How is this possible? But because Elijah is Elijah, he must be telling the truth!

Twenty minutes pass before the rabbi is able to regain a semblance of composure. He asks Elijah, "Well, then...*where is He? Where is the Messiah?*"

"Near the entrance to the city, consoling people in distress."

"But if he is with others, how will I recognize him?"

"He is covered with wounds, speaking words of compassion to unrepentant lepers."

During my studies in Rome, I visited the Pantheon. From the ancient stone floor, I gazed up at what seemed miles away: the *oculus*, the "eye," a small circular opening at the top of the structure. As sunlight streamed down from that distant opening, I remembered St. Benedict's experience of stars, galaxies, land, sea, and ocean—all enclosed within a single ray of a vast, limitless Light.

I related the light from that opening to the moment when Christ said, "God's rain—his goodness and radiant kindness—falls gently on the just and the unjust, on the righteous and the unrighteous."

I longed for the grace to pour that kind of kindness on others—regardless of who they were or what they might have done, or failed to do. I longed to mediate God's irrational compassion to the crucified of this world.

CHAPTER 4

Conversing with God without Armor

> Our images of God are not the same as our ideas about God....They are a powerful combination of thoughts and feelings....We may affirm that we believe in a God of love and grace, but our image of God may be of an abusive bully.
>
> —Juanita R. Ryan

1948. An old man is shuffling down a path of the former Bergen-Belsen death camp. He wonders how long he has been in the cemetery: Two hours? Three? Micah of Bratslav doesn't know. He feels disoriented. His unfounded fear of dementia starts to pry itself from deep inside his chest.

His parents are among the five thousand laid to rest in the cemetery. In deep distress, he yearns to speak with someone, but his only companion is a dense hush hanging over the paved paths, and the graves, so many graves.

◊

A month after his return from Germany, and six days before his eighty-fourth birthday, Micah vanishes. Family, friends, and villagers look everywhere. Has anyone seen him at the library? Not since Thursday. Has he visited his only remaining friend? No, he has not seen Micah for days. What about the synagogue?

The rabbi was speaking with Micah the day before when suddenly he looked scared and began to talk in a broken voice.

A day later, Micah's grandson, Aaron, receives information from a worker at a grocery store. She had asked Micah why he was loading so much into the back of a small truck. Was he going away?

"Yes. Into the forest."

After two days of searching in the forest, Aaron's inner compass guides him to an old slanted house. He's there, I know it, Aaron thinks. He inches toward the house, over earth sheathed with ice, like a man sneaking up on something.

Aaron knocks once. No answer. Then again. Still no answer.

After the third knock, the door opens, slowly, cautiously.

It's *him*!

A faint smile plays on his grandfather's lips. Aaron feels a rushing in his heart as he hugs him tight.

"What are you doing here, grandfather?"

Micah bends his head and says nothing. He gestures to his grandson to come in.

"Why didn't you tell us that you were going away?"

The old man shrugs his shoulders, but not in a disinterested way.

"Please," Aaron says, "speak to me. A sentence, a phrase, a word. *Anything.*"

Silence, dense. Brooding.

But…a few minutes later: "*Aaron?*"

Micah's lips start to quiver. In a tone so low that his grandson has to strain to hear him, this emerges from a dark space inside: "*I am afraid.*"

"Afraid? Of *what?*"

Micah corrects him. "Not of *what*, but of *Whom*."

"Who are you afraid of?"

"*God.*"

As the words vanish into the sounds of the forest, the lips of the old man seal again.

It will be a long time before he utters another word.

Rabbi Rachel Timoner says that in the ancient cultures from which Judaism emerged, gods resembled and acted like people. These fictional beings were depicted as having arms and legs, hands and genitals, a compulsion to be appeased, and the unsettling trait of unpredictability—bored and disinterested at one moment, vicious and wrathful at another. Even hungry orphans could be victims of the deity's fury. History witnesses to the influence of primitive cultures on whole populations, terrified by a fictional deity who—the people were convinced—demanded human sacrifice.

And Micah of Bratslav?

Perhaps he was afraid to face the God, who—to him—had remained as fascinated as a tourist while his parents were murdered.

But what if, when judging Micah, this God turned out to be wrathful? What then? *What would become of Micah of Bratslav?*

The failure to distinguish between God and those who do violence is often linked to the failure to remember—to look into the past and understand how the equation was formed: *violent man = violent God.* Perhaps after much struggle and pain, one might come to realize once and for all that *God is God and the violent are the violent.*

Elie Wiesel writes about a mother who has made a birthday cake for her five-year-old child. After dinner, she cuts the cake and lets out a sigh: if only her boy's little friends had been invited....

The father goes into a rage. This confuses the child, who wonders, *"What have I done wrong?"*

"Nothing," the mother assures him. "You have done nothing wrong. It's just that your father doesn't like strangers. *He likes only his own."*

After that, the child's birthday was no longer celebrated.

Imagine this father taking the boy to worship on Sunday. He hears *Our Father in heaven* and makes an association that sinks deep into his unconscious world...and stays there: *The Heavenly Father must be like dad.*

And thus, the equation: *uncaring, selfish father = uncaring, selfish Father.*

As an adult, he rejects *not God, but dad*—wrapped inside a distorted image.

Is it possible that many atheists are rejecting a fictitious and highly toxic image of God?

Think of someone who has been so consistently gentle and considerate, someone who cared about you so very much during your life, whose kindness and compassion came to you without a single reservation or condition.

Would you reject that person?

But God is infinitely more loving than the person who has most loved you.

If an atheist were to experience *the real Christ* and his gentle ways, do you suppose that the atheist would reject him?

In one of his books, Elie Wiesel describes the Selishter rabbi. He is standing over his shoulder, wondering, *Is he enriching the world with his words? Is he giving birth to angels by his deeds?**

Inevitably, silence brings persons like you, dear reader, and me to an awareness of a Secret Friend, who peers over our shoulders and, in various ways, asks these questions *without the slightest hint of judgment.*

---

* Elie Wiesel, *Legends of Our Time* (New York: Schocken, 2004), 31.

CHAPTER 5

If Your Attention Wanders

> If your attention wanders, return to prayer as soon
> as you notice your distraction, without lamenting
> over it....There will be days when the Office is a
> burden to you. On such occasions know how to
> offer your body, since your presence already signifies
> your desire...to praise your Lord. Believe in the
> presence of Christ within you even though you feel
> no tangible presence.
>
> —The Rule of Taizé

It has been said that alcoholism and other addictions are misdirected energy; that the goal of these compulsions is union with God.

A common expression in India is "monkey mind." The idea is that a monkey jumps from tree to tree, and from limb to limb, in search of greater satisfaction: bananas!

In the same way, the mind is in a state of incessant movement, ever searching for the God who is already present: "In him we live and move and have our being" (Acts 17:28).

Mind and body go hand in hand, so that when the mind settles down, the body settles down, and vice versa.

Stress is an overload on the senses and nervous system. Experiences such as physical and emotional strain, a terrifying event, or a sudden, loud noise leave an impression on the body.

Contemporary research discloses that when mind and body are settled, this creates the peaceful interior environment most conducive for the release of stress.

However, since the imprints of stress are lodged in the body, their release gives rise to bodily activity. Since mind and body resemble twins moving parallel to each other, the mind also becomes active.

This mental activity takes the form of thoughts or images: what have been called "distractions."

Cynthia Bourgeault, author of *Centering Prayer and Inner Awakening*, when asked if she thought that some breathing practice might be beneficial prior to starting the centering prayer session—something to calm a restless person walking into the house after a long workday—she answered, "Oh no, not at all. More restless means more thoughts. If my body could take it, I'd swallow twenty cups of coffee before starting Centering Prayer, just to get the thoughts rushing."

As I pondered the matter, her logic made sense. Each time we notice a thought or image that pulls us away from prayer, we are faced with a choice: either chase after the "distraction," or return to Christ. If this were to happen twenty times during a sitting, this would mean twenty opportunities to choose Christ. Such repeated choices, prayer session after prayer session, would gradually build a habit of returning to Jesus.

Why not understand a "distraction"—during public or private prayer—to be a sacred bell calling our attention back to Jesus? Interpreting these "intruders" in this way would help build a habit of traveling back to our center—Christ—during the circumstances of daily living.

CHAPTER 6

And God Spoke

God calls us in some ways to be his equals, to be so
united in Jesus that we become like God himself,
participating in his divine nature. This is the
Alliance, the New Covenant.

—Jean Vanier

Once upon a time, a Heavenly Voice spoke to the heart of a
devout Jewish goldsmith. The Silent Messenger said that *dabar*
was capable of gradually changing him into the likeness of God.
When the goldsmith realized what this meant, he was shaken,
"Me, an ordinary goldsmith, as gentle and compassionate as
God? No, *impossible!*"

One Sabbath later, his rabbi prefaced the public reading of
scripture by saying, "*And God spoke.*" When the goldsmith heard
that, he leaped to his feet and shouted, "*God speaks!* Do you
understand, my brothers and sisters? Can you believe that such
a miraculous thing could happen here: *God speaks!?*" The congregation was shocked. How was it possible that this ever-shy
goldsmith would behave in this way?

The goldsmith carried on so much that he had to be
escorted out of the synagogue, where he called out to passersby,
"God speaks! Can you believe that such a miraculous thing
could happen? *God speaks!*"

Through *dabar*.

Meaning literally "word," *dabar* defies translation. But this Hebrew term means far more than sound or meaning. *Dabar* is divine, creative, life-sustaining, and life-giving energy, a transforming power come to us from beyond.

It may arrive at any moment, as in Scripture or through the sudden appearance of a homeless stranger. It may manifest in spontaneous hospitality or in an ancient Gregorian melody sung in a wintry church in Rome.

When the Book of Genesis recalls the first event of creation on *yom ehad*, "day one," it is in terms of *dabar*, a mother who gives birth by saying, "Let there be light." Elsewhere, the psalmist declares that *dabar* created the heavens, and through the power of *dabar*, they continue to breathe. The joy of fire and hail, he chants, is to "fulfill" *dabar*, who gathers the waters of every sea as in a flask, and in her kindness, spreads out snow like wool, and scatters frost like ashes.

Dabar is the ecstasy of a woman who nourishes and sustains her offspring. She is intelligent: all she does is for the purpose of transforming us into the likeness of God—which is what she was gradually doing in the life of the desert father, Anastasius, when...

One day the old man entered his hut and discovered that his Bible was missing. When the robber—a man who had visited him—went to sell the book, the buyer said, "Leave it with me, so that I can be sure it's worth the sixteen pence you're asking for it."

The buyer took the Bible to Anastasius.

"Do you think this is worth sixteen pence?"

"Yes."

When the buyer told the robber about his meeting with Anastasius, the man's dark, intense eyes widened.

"That's all he said? Nothing more? You're sure?"

"No, nothing else. Why? Have you changed your mind?"

"*Yes*," the robber said, snatching the Bible out of the buyer's hands. "I've changed my mind!" He rushed through the streets, into the wilderness. Once inside Abba Anastasius's dwelling, the robber hurled himself at the old man's feet.

"Forgive me," he said, tears streaming down his face. "I didn't know what I was doing. Take the Bible back, please!"

"Peace be with you, my son. Come, rise to your feet. Of course I forgive you. As for the Bible, I want you to have it as a gift—that you may come to know the unconditional kindness of Christ, and the power of his *dabar*."

The psalmist sings of Someone, who "sends forth" his word—a messenger who "runs quickly." The Holy One leaves it up to each messenger to make up her own disguise, and to sing her own song, in her own way.

His sole concern is that, when heard, *dabar* might awaken a spark of paradise in the heart of the friend of God.

And an angel be born into the world.

CHAPTER 7

The Word Carries Us
Wherever We Go

When a person says the words of prayer…an
awesome silent fire takes hold of him. Then he
knows not where he is; he cannot see, he cannot
hear. All this happens in a flash of an instant—as he
ascends beyond the world of time.

—from *Your Word Is Fire:*
The Hasidic Masters on Contemplative Prayer,
edited by Arthur Green and Barry W. Holtz

Since The Great Blue Heron is all-knowing, he takes in the entire
body of humankind in one glance. When he speaks his *dabar* to
someone, he is also speaking in a deeply personal way to each
unique cell of that universal body. *Dabar* arrives with the precise
word I need at a given stage of my journey. But I have to do more
than "read" *dabar*. I'm called to listen to its song in faith, as to
someone I love.

With the scriptural text open, I linger over a sentence.
Eventually its words vanish into the furthest limits of my second heart. I hold still for a long time, eyes closed, as the sentence repeats itself over and over, barely audible, so gentle. That

sentence will carry me during the day, as I listen to it again and again.

○

Abba Anthony wanted to test some of the desert fathers who came to visit him. He suggested a text from the Scriptures and asked each to explain its meaning.

All spoke, but Abba Joseph kept silent.

"And you," Anthony said, "What do you have to say?"

"Nothing," Joseph said. "I have nothing to say. *I don't know.*"

Anthony looked steadily at the desert fathers and said, "See, of all of you, Abba Joseph is the only one who knows the way, *because he does not know.*"

Dabar engages the whole person, beginning at the level of "not knowing": a loving silence far beneath concepts or images. From there, it sweeps into our feelings, imagination, senses.

When we listen to *dabar* in this way and flow with the fragrance of its wisdom, we become *dabar*—so that gradually every scriptural word becomes our *dabar*. Then every crownlet of every sacred letter begins to express our depth, flowing from the Heart of a Greater Depth.

We become the Speaker in his abyss of love, and his secret sound, and the listener too.

By becoming *dabar*, we flow deeper into the center of a feast in the wilderness—where every living thing is a friend, spiraling in concentric circles inside the Depth of the Great Round Dance.

How good it is to be the *dabar* of the Great Blue Heron, whose Gentle Hands cover the planets in all the galaxies! How good to be *dabar*, roaring through canyons and hills, and the silence of the human heart!

CHAPTER 8

Christ, Imagination and the Gospels

> Using my imagination wasn't so much making
> things up, as it was trusting that my imagination
> could help to lead me to the One who created
> it....That didn't mean that everything I imagined
> during prayer was coming from God. But it did
> mean that from time to time, God could use my
> imagination as one way of communicating with me.
>
> —Fr. James Martin, SJ

After Gandhi was assassinated, two items were found in his room: a portrait of Christ and a threadbare bible. How many times had Gandhi turned page after page of this sacred book, day after day, year after year? Hundreds of times? Thousands? More? Surely this serious assimilation of the Gospels had to have contributed mightily to his teaching on nonviolence.

It is fitting that, as you step onto the grounds of the Martin Luther King Center in Atlanta, you find a statue of Gandhi. It welcomes you to a place that celebrates a man who had ventured into the land of likeness and changed, over time, into kindness incarnate.

In the seventies, while at an interreligious meeting, I was introduced to the revered Buddhist teacher Tatsani Roshi. He claimed a strong familiarity with the Gospels.

At a late afternoon meeting, Br. Eusebius, a young monk, was trying to prove a point by quoting from the Gospels. He read it in a monotone voice, "My God, my God, why have you abandoned me?"

Tatsani Roshi intervened, *"Christ didn't say that!"*

"What do you mean, Christ didn't say that?"

Eusebius read it again, once more in a flat monotone.

"He didn't say that!"

"Well then, what *did* he say?"

Tatsani Roshi rose slowly to his feet and paused for a few seconds before roaring, "MY GOD, MY GOD, WHY HAVE YOU FORSAKEN ME?"

Silence. A few nervous coughs.

"That's what he said."

Like Gandhi, Tatsani Roshi lived the Gospels.

One way of doing this is through the traditional practice of *lectio divina*; another is the Ignatian method of using the imagination to pray the Gospels. Both practices are offered to us as gifts for our inner journey. It's up to us to discern—together with the Spirit—which one fits.

Here is a story that draws our attention to the power of imagination.

The Menninger Clinic was conducting a test that included children with cancer. One of them was a young boy with an inoperable brain tumor. The child was asked to visualize a laser from Star Wars, and to imagine it destroying the tumor. Time went by, and so did a number of tests. However, because they showed no improvement, the boy's parents decided to stop the experiment. But the child continued his visualization.

One day he fell down a flight of stairs and was taken to a hospital for x-rays. A doctor familiar with the child's case was stunned when he saw the results. *The cancer had disappeared!*

The doctor said, "*It looks like it has been cut out with a laser beam!*"

Today, the faculty of imagination is not taken as seriously as in the era of the Jewish Scriptures, when God spoke to prophets through the vivid imagery of a dream. However, it remains true that imagination evokes creative power sufficient to produce not only great works of art, music, and literature, but also science and technology as well.

The unconscious does not know the difference between what we imagine and what is real. Images glide into the unconscious and, from that unseen world, impact us in a variety of ways.

Were we to imagine ourselves as Christ in a gospel scene, the unconscious would assume that this *really was happening*; and we would feel that it *was* happening.

By identifying with the outcasts of society in gospel scenes, we might come to experience, rather than merely understand, Christ's paradigm of radical equality and inclusivity.

Imaginative praying of the Gospels excludes detached observation, "I am watching myself doing this or listening to myself thinking that."

The Harvard University professor Tulku Thondup shares a memory of a music teacher with a wonderful, trained voice... and a fear of her weekly duties as cantor at the local synagogue.

One Sabbath before a service, she wept so violently that she realized how crippling her fear, or terror, had become. In time, she found a quiet place where she began to imagine herself leading the service skillfully, singing in a way that felt good to her without being overly worried about the melodies she found so hard to practice.

This music teacher imagined what it would feel like to be confident about her singing. In her interior world, she heard the beautiful sound of her voice, which eventually delighted the congregation. She felt an expansive sense of gladness and inspiration over being able to share that music.

As in the case of the music teacher, it can happen that images may open us up to additional or alternative perspectives of experience and action, and to the replacement of stagnant, fixed, confining notions. This process may lead to greater contact with our feelings at more profound levels—a connection that has the potential to summon the energies we have at our disposal, to bring more life to ourselves and to others.

The author Timothy M. Gallagher, OMV, writes about a woman who, as she imaginatively entered a gospel scene, at one time wondered whether "anything will happen."

However, she had learned that *patience and trust* are necessary if imaginative prayer is to bear fruit: the patience of continuing fidelity to this prayer, and trust that God does change us in this process.

This woman had also learned to recognize the space "that allows me to enter the surface of the text and *go in*."

Another lesson learned: everyone has her or his own unique way of using this method. Nobody is bound by a map to be followed.

Imagination in Scripture

Spend it all, shoot it, play it, lose it, all, right away.
Do not hoard what seems good for a later place....
Give it, give it all, give now....Anything you do not
give freely and abundantly becomes lost to you. You
open your safe and find ashes.

—Annie Dillard

To prepare for sacred reading, please close your eyes and thank the Spirit of Jesus for what he is going to do in your life through your imaginative interaction with the Gospel. In this way, you will thank him for that blessing *before* he blesses: an expression of deep trust and confidence.

Read the text you have chosen (or, more accurately, *listen* to the one that the Spirit has chosen for you).

Invite the Spirit to draw you into the gospel scene, and explore it, as thoroughly as you can, with the imaginative senses.

Let's imagine a scene: Someone turns to you and whispers something. What is he saying? Suppose that Christ notices your exchange. How do you feel when you realize that he is looking at you? What might Christ be thinking?

What if he starts to walk toward you? How do you feel as he draws closer?

Drawing on this scenario with college students one day, I asked how they felt about Christ walking toward them.

A student said, "I was scared."

But why be afraid? Was it because of an illusory image of Christ that depicted him *as he was not*—as a menacing figure?

In its own time and pace, the student's imagination helped her to pray over her impression of Christ. Gradually, she felt empowered to move forward, equipped with a greater truth about who Jesus is.

She thought: *Why should I fear someone who healed paralytics and the blind? Why be scared of the One who invited sinners to his party, without demanding that they change? Why tremble when he passes by, on his way to die for love?*

If you *become* Jesus in a gospel scene, what does that feel like?

As Jesus, what do you make of the situation confronting you? What is going through your mind? How does it feel to be Jesus, helping someone? How does it feel to listen as Jesus did, and still does—with deep reverence?

To become Jesus in a scene is to deepen our identity as Christ, by participation. Please remember—the unconscious doesn't realize the difference between you and Jesus!

St. Ignatius Loyola would have us move from active imagination of a gospel scene to conversation. His spirituality revolves around the Spanish word *conversar*—"to talk with": a sincere, respectful dialogue.

During the conversation, Christ's voice will rise quite gently and begin to speak within you. Then listen to whatever words rise up from your inner space. They are *your* words, addressed to Jesus.

Let the conversation flow back and forth, back and forth...
Easily, gently, and without effort.

In faith, believe that you are exchanging thoughts and feelings with Jesus, as friend to Friend.

You will know when the conversation has ended.

Thank Jesus for drawing you closer to him through his eagerness to *conversar*.

Close your eyes, and breathe God.

Tales Heard at Low Tide

A story, we believe, and perhaps we are out of fashion here, should exert a moral force, should charge and illuminate. Like light, it must have direction, intensity, and color.

—John Dufresne

CHAPTER 1

Moshe

As the Baal Shem lay upon the bottom of the Vessel, a lone and silent Thing, a Heavenly Voice, rose quite gently and began to speak within him, first simply, and as at home, but always swelling, and becoming mightier, until at last the Voice swallowed the howling of the ocean that was lost as a whisper within her call. And the Master drank the sound of the Voice of God.

—Meyer Levin, in *Classic Hassidic Tales*

It was a beautiful Swiss summer day when I first saw him: a man with ruddy cheeks, wearing a black hat and shell-rimmed glasses. His eyes were radiant.

He was more than an old man strolling through a dense crowd of tourists and window shoppers in Interlaken. He was more than the silence I sensed as he passed by a shop and greeted the shopkeeper and me. He was more than the black I saw as he moved slowly into the distance, this old man in his black suit and tie, tipping his black hat to the old woman at the fruit stand.

I watched him until the faintest sign of his silence had moved on, leaving not a trace of black to linger behind.

I turned to Helmut, the shopkeeper.

"Who was that—the man in black who greeted us a minute ago?"

"That's Moshe. Look. Let me show you."

He pulled out a piece of paper and wrote, "*Rebbe.*"

"Reh–bee," Helmut said, smiling, with a trace of indulgence in his voice. "A spiritual master—Jewish."

"You know him?"

"Yes. When he came here, I was confused. I had trouble sleeping, and my marriage was going from bad to worse. I questioned everything. I knew I had to talk with someone; I had been searching for something deeper, more essential—and finding nothing. It was like going through those Chinese boxes, one inside another, on and on, always coming up empty-handed. Do you understand?"

I nodded.

"When I met Moshe, I knew instinctively that he had been sent here by God—to listen to me, and of course to others in need. So I asked him if we might get together. Immediately, I felt a rush of kindness and compassion—his. He said 'absolutely— when? This afternoon? What time?'"

"He sounds like an *abba*," I said.

"*Abba?*"

"An elder in the desert father tradition."

"Desert father?"

"The desert fathers were the first Christian monks. They lived in the fourth century…"

The shopkeeper cut me off in mid-sentence.

"I don't want to hear about Christians. Do you understand? Tell me, over the centuries, how many Jews do you suppose that Christians killed, without the slightest trace of guilt? Millions? Hundreds of millions? At Good Friday services, you referred to us as the perfidious Jews. It was said officially that the Jews of the present day carried the guilt of *deicide*—the murder of God, the killing of Christ. When Hitler's inner circle met to decide on the final solution, someone said that at least two camps would never object: the Arabs and the Christians. So, both were accomplices in the Holocaust."

I tried to get hold of myself, but for a good while could not. My hands were shaking.

"Nervous?"

Helmut was looking at me with a sneer of disdain.

"Yes, and much more."

"Oh?"

With my voice quivering, I asked if Moshe felt the way Helmut did about Christians.

"He was imprisoned at Auschwitz. When the Allies liberated the camp, he prayed *kaddish*: the prayer for the dying, and the dead. He did not seek revenge against the SS guards who had been captured."

Helmut had asked Moshe why this was so.

"Because I am living the teachings of the Baal Shem Tov."

The Baal Shem Tov, or Besht, was a great spiritual teacher in the Jewish mystical tradition.

According to Abraham Heschel, the Besht felt that the Jew's relationship with God was a romance. It bothered him to notice that many rituals had become routine and exercises in repetition instead of gestures of surprise. The Baal Shem Tov's soul was strong, gentle, and deep.

Moshe liked nothing better than to tell one story after another related to this saint. But he didn't just tell stories. He became the tales. When he finished, he seemed not to know where he was. At various times I tried to get him to talk about Auschwitz, but he would always change the subject—such as the time he spoke with passion about the Rebbe who, once a year, would sit in his room at night and receive his disciples. You know how? By listening to their voices, flowing into his ears from the four ends of the earth. He insisted he wasn't talking about himself, that this was from the Hasidic tradition, but I am sure that Moshe was talking about Moshe.

One of Moshe's favorite stories had to do with Dov Ber—also known as the Maggid of Mezritch—a man so fiercely addicted to himself that he could see only through an inner window of judgments and fixed beliefs.

People trembled when they saw him. A Talmudic scholar, he did not permit himself to laugh or even smile. The Maggid of Mezritch believed fervently in self-inflicted pain, but eventually his addiction to penance caught up with him. He fell seriously ill, and doctors could do nothing more. As a last hope, someone suggested, "Why not see the Baal Shem Tov?"

Even though the Maggid disapproved of the visionary's path—the Besht sought to alleviate suffering, while the Maggid was sure that life should be a struggle—he gave in.

It was midnight when the Baal Shem Tov, dressed in a coat of wolf fur turned inside out, handed the Maggid the Book of Splendor. Dov Ber read aloud for a page when the Besht suddenly interrupted.

"Something is missing," he said. "Something is lacking in your knowledge."

"What is that?"

"*Soul.*"

From that point on, the room was a mass of Fire. Light extended from wall to wall—a radiance that had been present all along, secretly watching the Maggid read.

After two hours of this—two hours at the center of creation—the Maggid got up to leave.

"Wait," the Besht said. "I won't let you go without a blessing."

And Israel Baal Shem Tov, the Master of the Good Name, bent his head to receive a blessing.

◊

Soul. If you are from New Orleans, as I am, you know what the word means—not intellectually, or through the emotions, but by an intuition that rises up from the second level of the heart.

I would tell you that *soul* is at your fingertips, in your chest, in the soles of your feet. It is spiritual energy, beyond definition or description. You simply experience it, not as an object, but from within outwards. Jazz, the blues, and spirituals are packed with *soul.* So are moments of deep meaning: births and deaths, weddings and burials, a spiritual breakthrough. The silence of the bush in New Guinea, where a primitive might stand for hours listening to the wind, has *soul.*

And God *is* Soul.

◊

Seven Hasidic masters are seated around a table in the House of Study. The Maggid of Mezritch, now a successor of the Baal Shem Tov, is praying the Scriptures in another room—*with soul!*

A door opens. The Maggid appears, radiant with the light of Sinai. Terrified, five of the teachers run into the streets. A sixth hides under a table. Only Rebbe Wolfe stands his ground, applauding the scene with gusto.

CHAPTER 2

A Dream

This is a tale with a kernel.
You'll have to use your own teeth to crack it.
—Charles Simic

I am living in a wilderness of glaciers and geysers, a wasteland where my companions are rugged coasts and canyons and rocks—thousands and thousands of rocks.

Christ showed up here long ago and stayed. This is where he confronted the stranger dressed in a costume of dragon scales gleaming in the dark. It was a good disguise, but Christ knew better.

"Just bread?" he said. "People live by more than bread...."

Blessed be the rocks of this land.
Blessed be the Great Blue Heron,
who watches over the bent trees,
whose blind eyes send blessings to all beings,
near or far away.

A conversation, overheard by three whooper swans, on a day just born:

Chris, an American, tells his host, "I feel as though I'm being watched."

Gunnar raises his eyebrows.

"I don't know what it is. Maybe the position of the sun, or the lack of vegetation, but wherever I go, I feel as though I'm being watched."

"What you just said amazes me," Gunnar says. "Not because you notice this, but since you've noticed it so *quickly*. You're experiencing what everyone here senses—sooner or later."

Chris stares at his friend.

"I was a child when I first felt that the rocks were watching me. It was a physical experience, actually quite comforting—the unmistakable sense that a delicate presence was tending to me."

"And so, Gunnar, the *rocks* are watching? I find it hard to swallow that!"

"More than the rocks, my friend. You may know that Tolkien did the research for his trilogy here. The natives believe that the first inhabitants of this country are watching. The hobbits are looking out of the rocks…"

"*Gunnar, be serious!*"

"Hobbits, or whatever you choose to call them. Let's say hobbit-like creatures: friendly, small, and mischievous—they love to play tricks on people. It's not unusual for them to break into houses and run off with food. Some say they eat as much as six times a day. I don't know, I haven't seen them, only felt them all around, watching."

Hobbits? *Just hobbits?* Or is Gunnar conveying an experience in terms familiar to his culture? Is he conscious of a vaster, deeper Presence, of which the rocks and hobbits are symbols?

Perhaps Gunnar is sensing an intense, loving awareness that pervades every pocket of creation—a spaciousness without father or mother, a kernel singing quietly, no notes missing.

When—in another time, another culture—the psalmist felt this same Presence watching him, he took up his harp and sang back:

> You know when I sit down and when I rise up;
>> you discern my thoughts from far away.
> If I ascend to heaven, you are there;
>> if I make my bed in Sheol, you are there.
>>>> (Ps 139: 2, 8)

In midafternoon, at a distance, I catch sight of what looks like a body of soft down. I draw closer. An eider duck is sitting in her nest, staring at me from several feet away. I wonder what would happen if I went over there.

When I reach the nest, I extend my hand, slowly, to touch her beak. The duck does not draw back. Instead, she closes her eyes: a delicate symbol of the silence that connects her with me, and the friendship she offers—and receives—in this wasteland where everything and everyone is a friend who whispers, "*Namaste.*"

It could not be otherwise. This is the place Christ loves; his home: the unaccountable fragrance of the rocks, the wind glittering in the dark.

Praying in the shadows, the final verse of a psalm begins to stir inside me, like *canto hondo*—the deep song of the gypsies of Andalusia. I find myself leaning into the rhythm, knowing that when the last note has vanished into silence, another leaf will be living on the "tree" that is "myself."

"The Maker of heaven and earth," the last psalm ends—the Creator of *yom ehad*, the first day of creation: a time when everything was in God's womb—and yet out of the womb, moments when whatever was, was—and yet flowed in the Heart of God.

This is what the Hebrew Bible calls the first stirring of creation. It speaks of a formless wilderness, of darkness, of light. The only sign of life is *ruah*: a wind, a Divine Presence soaring over the waters.

The wings of *ruah* are still swaying over the waters of this wilderness I call home. *Yom ehad* is still here, in this desert of rocks, Christ's sanctuary, where the first lines of the Book of Genesis are being written—and rewritten—every day: *God created everyone in his image and likeness....*

Tonight, the rays of the full moon are gleaming over the purple and rust of the rocks. Normally, we see just one side of the moon. But tonight its barren spaces have rotated so that both edges are peeking down at me as I stand still, learning to wait.

◊

Everything in creation is a kernel inside a tale: a quince blossom opening up, revealing its unspoken language, an energy that glides quietly, the way the Great Blue Heron ascends into the heavens, without making a sound.

Vaster than the spheres, older than the canyons of the west and the mountains of the east, this Heron is the Luminous Source of blind trees and deep hollows; and of the kindness that hums through the wind on a solitary night in the wilderness, where after years of radical change, a friend of God continues his journey through the land of likeness.

◊

In this wilderness of glaciers and geysers, and thousands and thousands of rocks, someone turns to her neighbor and says, "*You would think that with every passing second this wilderness would be closer to day two!*"

But it isn't. Nor will it happen tomorrow, or the day after, or ever.

Here it will always be day one.

CHAPTER 3

A Christ of the Soul

The saints are what they are, not because their
sanctity makes them admirable to others, but
because the gift of sainthood makes it possible for
them to admire everyone else.

—Thomas Merton

After reading a four-paragraph piece in Theophane Boyd's *Tales
of a Magic Monastery*, my imagination takes over—again. It
encourages me to create a story based on what I have just read.
Nothing sprawling, no epic production; just something simple,
with a single point. I begin to write but not before first thanking
the Spirit for guiding my pen, the result being what follows.

◊

I'm a graduate student on spring break. Instead of vaca-
tioning with friends in Florida, I make my third retreat at what
has become, for me, a spiritual home.

During each visit, I watch Br. Ezekiel closely, as he walks into
the church to join his brothers for the Liturgy. He is mindfulness
in motion, each move and gesture grounded in reverence, at ease
with all that is. Tall and straight, his broad shoulders fill out the
upper part of his black monastic robe.

With a narrow smile, Fr. Daniel, the guest master, describes
Ezekiel, "He assimilates the New Testament in Greek and the

Jewish Scriptures in Hebrew. As his favorite poet, Cesar Vallejo, would depict him, 'Ezekiel is a Christ of the soul.' His inner life is mighty deep."

Fr. Daniel is addicted to storytelling. It's not hard to prod out of him a tale of a time when, long ago, Ezekiel walked into the scriptorium and noticed three monks reading at a table: the men who had plotted the ouster of the abbot, a man of prayer whom Ezekiel loved and respected.

Ezekiel's wound over the abbot's forced resignation was raw and fresh, and his anger no trifle. When he came across the three monks, something snapped. Whirling around, he walked rapidly to the church and yanked the abbot's long, thick crozier into his hands.

In the scriptorium, Ezekiel stood in front of the terrified monks, clutching the crozier above his head, and then, raising his leg, cracked it into two pieces over his thigh. Then he hurled the fragments onto the table.

"There," he said. "*It's finished!* What you have done cannot be undone."

I ask to meet Br. Ezekiel.

"I'm of Sicilian ancestry," he says, after shaking my hand. "The Sicilian way of doing things is in my blood: *straight to the point.* Candor enters every conversation and never leaves until it's over. I would expect the same now."

No preliminary small talk, no easing into the subject—just right into the question, "*Why do you want to see me?*"

I explain that I have been considering a monastic vocation.

"*I?* You mean, *on your own?*"

"With God, of course."

"In mind or in heart? Or both?"

No words emerge from my lips.

Br. Ezekiel pauses before putting another question to me. "What is your spiritual practice?"

"What do you mean, spiritual practice?"

"How do you *not do*, to dispose yourself to be pulled deeper into the Great Heart, who lives at the bottom of your soul?"

Confused, I say that I think about God a lot, read about the life of Christ...

Ezekiel cuts me off.

"ABOUT? *About* is not enough, lad! What you are describing is the necessary horizontal. But where is the essential vertical? I detect no sign of a willingness to commit yourself to a spiritual practice that will take you deep."

Again, I don't know what to say.

Br. Ezekiel looks into my eyes. His gaze is gentle, warm, and I think, compassionate.

And yet...all of a sudden he jumps to his feet and shouts: "NOW! Do you hear me? NOW!"

You can imagine how shocked I am.

"*Now* is the time to read the Prologue to the *Rule of St. Benedict!*"

It takes me more than a few seconds to gain a semblance of composure.

"I'm not a monk," I say, weakly.

"You are a human being who must read the part Benedict wrote for *you: NOW is the time to rouse yourself from emotional and spiritual sleep! NOW is the time to open your eyes to the Deifying Light!*"

I begin to wonder, *Is Br. Ezekiel all there?*

"He wrote that for me? But he lived in the fifth century!"

"That's right. He lived in clock time, but also...at the bottom of a soul that, at its furthest edge, opens out into the *no-time* of infinity—just like your spirit and mine."

I clear my throat.

"I'll have to think about all of this, Brother."

"Lad, you live too much in the head. You analyze, sort out, and argue with yourself over point A, as opposed to point B."

How does he know me so well? In graduate school, I'm expected to do much thinking.

"Until now," Ezekiel says, "you have been exploring one blind alley after another. But at least you have not bought totally into the cultural consensus that our value and identity depend on what we accomplish and on what other people think of us. I say not totally—but you are edging toward buying into it one hundred percent. You are in danger, lad. Wake up! NOW!"

So how does he know *that*? This is our first time together!

Ezekiel pauses before going on.

"Because, to a large extent, you are entangled in that fictitious consensus, you are convinced that you have to *do* something—by yourself, apart from God—to figure out your path in life. But don't you realize that if *for one second* you were separate from God, you would cease to exist? You don't realize that a sacred road is waiting for you—a path that will help you to perceive, listen, and love exactly the way God does."

"I don't understand."

"Then find that passage in the Prologue about waking up, and let it sink into the center of your being, where you are united with Christ. The passage carries with it a special grace. A *powerful* grace. Before you leave, see Fr. Eusebius. He'll give you a copy of the Prologue, and might help you to find a spiritual practice that fits your unique makeup. He's a wise elder. Don't wait!"

I walk out of the room without saying goodbye. Instead of looking for Fr. Eusebius, I go home.

◊

For a year, that word—*NOW!*—follows me around, especially in dreams that depict me on the verge of starting on a wide road, then pulling back. One night, Ezekiel appears in a vivid dream and says, "You're dissatisfied with your life. And you *know it*, but don't want to do anything other than think about options and possibilities. How many times do I have to tell you to welcome—and internalize—that passage in the Prologue? Time is running out, lad. Wake up, open your eyes to the Light, get onto that sacred road and start to take tiny steps toward thinking the way God does!"

Somehow, with my defenses down during sleep, Ezekiel's words fall beneath my resistances, and land deep in my soul. Something is starting to burst into a thousand threads.

I'd like to tell you what happened after that, but it's hard to put into words. All I can say is that over time, I gradually reached the point of wanting to begin the odyssey.

And I did!

Now I'm encouraging people to join me. *And they're listening!*

I must tell you that the other day I was taken aback when I heard *now* inside me. I can assure you that it wasn't Br. Ezekiel! So then who could it have been? Was it the vulnerable, sensitive child inside me or the Great Spirit?

At this critical point, Br. Ezekiel appears in my imagination.

I hardly recognize his voice. It is so gentle and low! He says, "It's not one or the other, lad. It's both!"

Silence before he continues.

"Two longings have joined to become one desire. Isn't it wonderful? You and the Spirit are singing, in two-part harmony, about that section of Benedict's Prologue...and about the odyssey you two are sharing as you make your way through the land of likeness!"

CHAPTER 4

The Little House

He sold the slave to a local slave buyer by the name
of Bart Jenkins....Once the contract is signed, (the
slave) is utterly beyond reach and beyond help as if
buried alive. Having completed his purchase, Bart
Jenkins came in the night, and knocked the man on
the head while he was asleep, and bound him, and
led him away with a rope.

—Wendell Berry

Sometimes I remember how it felt to be six, growing up in New
Orleans in one of those big and ancient houses surrounded by
bigger and more ancient homes.

A little wooden house, brown and badly neglected, sat at
the far edge of the property. My sister thought it looked lonely.
My brother warned me never to go near it.

"Why not?"

"Because it's haunted, *or so I'm told.*"

If that were true, it didn't scare Lilly, our black maid.
During the day, when no one was around, I would see her go
into the little house and stay a while.

◊

I can't explain why this happened, but toward the end of
my sixth year, at least twice each day, I would lean against our

banana tree in the backyard and stare at the little house. My family thought, *There he goes again, daydreaming!*

After six weeks, I was no longer staring at the tiny wooden building. Now I felt as though *I was keeping it company*.

The autumn night was long when, unable to sleep, I went outside by the banana tree and gazed at it. But quite abruptly it felt as though a scythe was starting to slide toward me. I ran to my room and locked the door. I was terrified.

The next morning, I told Lilly what had happened. Knitting her eyebrows, she stood still for a long moment.

"I've seen you go into the little house, Lilly."

She braced.

"Now, don't you *ever* tell your parents that you've seen me do that. They've warned me to stay away."

"Lilly, I'm curious. It's an old house. Who used to live there?"

"Child, you've been on this earth for more than six years, and in all that time you never wondered who used to live there?"

I shrugged my shoulders. "I don't know. I just thought it was just a house that nobody paid attention to. I didn't get interested in it until this year."

Lilly waved me into a chair, sat across from me and kept quiet. While the clock was striking five times, I noticed that her eyes looked blurred and moist.

"The little house used to be the slave quarters."

I had no idea what a slave was. Lilly couldn't believe that.

"Let's go to the sofa," she said. "Nobody's around, so I reckon it might be time to tell you a few things."

Lilly said that the little house was the reason she had applied to work here.

"Why did you want to do that?"

"I'll tell you later…*maybe*."

Lilly told a story about a Jewish child who walked into his grandfather's den late one afternoon, sobbing.

"*Yehiel, what's wrong?*"

The child said that he had played hide and seek with his friends. When his turn came, he hid. An hour passed, but nobody showed up.

"*They went home and left me there...*"

With tears in his eyes, the old man took his grandson into his arms.

"God, too, is weeping, my dear Yehiel. God too is hiding, waiting, but so few are looking for him. Do you realize how much that must hurt him?"

I didn't understand how that story connected with the little house. Lilly did her best to explain.

"For years that house has been weeping, since nobody has tried to find out what went on in there. Nobody knows the way people died in that house—before they died."

Lilly said that in Africa a long time ago, white men forced families onto slave ships. I was shocked to hear that even children were chained to long planks in the hull.

"Many died during the voyage," Lilly said. "Nobody took away the corpses, or the stench and the diseases."

After the ship arrived in New Orleans, crude hands drove survivors into the slave mart in the French Quarter. Children watched, with eyes grown ancient during the voyage. They stood terrified as a man decided who of them would make a good slave, and who would not.

The procedure was eerily reminiscent of the "selection" conducted by the Nazi doctor, Josef Mengele, after the arrival of

Jews at a death camp. If he waved a baton to the right, it meant that a prisoner was fit for work. When the baton swung to the left, the captive went to his death.

/\

I felt strong nausea and fear as I imagined slaves screaming while their families were split up: the father sold to one slaveholder, the mother to another, the children to still another.

"A slaveholder on this property bought a mother, father, and one of the children, and let the other two children get sold to someone else."

"*How do you know all that, Lilly?*"

"Because in New Orleans, some of us black folks know our history: who was sold and to whom. Child, listen to what I'm going to tell you—and don't you *ever* repeat it to anyone: *The father, mother, and child who lived in the little house were my ancestors. That's why I wanted to work here; to be near the little house.*"

/\

I went to bed early that night. In my sleep, my legs kicked all the sheets onto the floor during a nightmare in which I saw myself chained to a long plank in the hull of a slave ship next to a decaying corpse.

Five hours later, I bolted up in bed, shivering. After a long time, I felt strong enough to get up and go outside.

I leaned against the banana tree and closed my eyes. The atmosphere surrounding me pulsed quiet and alive.

I stayed that way for a while, until a thought sprang up: *Are you going to do it?*

I knew what that meant. *Are you going to visit the little house?*

I felt a fluttering in the stomach.

After ten minutes, I took a deep breath and started to walk slowly toward the house.

I stopped a few feet from the entrance and stared. My heart beat fast.

I took another deep breath, followed by another.

I inched toward the door. My right hand rested on the cold knob for a few moments. Then I turned it very, very slowly.

I stepped inside and stood still in the dark. The silence was mighty strong.

I could have turned on the light, but didn't want to.

Then... *Was it my imagination, or was it real?*

I felt quiet as I sensed tender arms embracing me.

I started to cry.

Someone was holding me gentle and close, whispering into my ear, "No need to cry, sweet child, no need to cry. We saw you watching day after day, and now you've come at last. Would you stay a while and pray with us?"

CHAPTER 5

As the Angel of Death Drew Near

Nigger-owning makes the rich man proud and ugly
and makes the poor man mean. It's a curse laid on
the land. We've lit a fire and now it's burning us
down. God is going to liberate niggers, and fighting
to prevent it is against God. Did you own any?
—Charles Frazier

They were sure that the end was certain and nigh. The wheel of
nonviolence had just turned another notch, and everything had
looked so much more hopeful. Things were moving ahead,
momentum gained.

Optimism had shifted into the minds and hearts of civil
rights workers and other noble souls throughout the country,
black and white.

Then news ripped into the air: *Martin Luther King has been
killed. It happened at a....*

Many, who had espoused the way of nonviolence, regressed
to the days of tangle and curse. The venom of that killing did far
more than split the black heart in two.

It was a dangerous time to live in a city.

I, a white man, lived in a city.

I taught in an upper-class Catholic high school—all
white, save for two whose skin was of a different color. I began

to wonder if some of the students sensed that, at any moment, they might be forced to drink death's wine, as might I.

◊

A week into the first semester, four Brothers and I sat in the faculty lounge pondering the wisdom of attending our opening football game in a black neighborhood.

"Are we temporarily insane for even *thinking* about going?"

"We're going there to witness."

"Witness? *To what?*"

"To our loyalty to the team and the school. How would it look if only our students and none of the Brothers or lay teachers went?"

After an hour of discussion, it's unanimous: *We're going.*

◊

As we draw near to our destination, a sentence stumbles past Br. Jacob's lips, *"It's not too late to turn around."*

The only response is a nervous cough coming from the back seat.

Another mile and...*there it is.*

Br. Celsus says, "The stadium. Are you guys *sure* you want to do this?"

Nobody says anything.

A few blocks later, we are walking toward the stadium.

Br. Jacob rubs his eyes. Allergies.

But I bet that if I had shaken his hand, the palm would have been *wet.*

◊

As we enter the stadium, my eyes fix their gaze on a tall black student in yellow pants.

Suddenly it's *figure-ground*. The crowd melts into the background as the student shifts into the foreground. In my awareness, *only he exists*.

My heart starts to beat fast. *What's going on?*

After the game, we drive a block. Br. Neil shouts, "*LOOK!*"

Black teenagers are chasing one of our students. They are not far behind. Br. Kevin and I leap out of the car and rush toward the student, making furious gestures: *Hurry! Back to the car!*

It's incredible. The boy *stops* to inform us that he dropped his book bag "back there." It was just enough time for the teenagers to catch up with him...and us. We are encircled.

It is as though a neighborhood loudspeaker had announced the capture of the prey. Men, women, and children pour out of row houses. As they rush toward us, they shout from afar, "*KILL THEM! KILL THEM!*"

Vocal chords swell. The neighborhood has turned into the ancient Roman Coliseum: hungry lions roaring, people screaming for blood.

A ritual born minutes after Dr. King was assassinated.

Not having heard about the murder, a white motorist driving in or near a black neighborhood is stopped and yanked from his car. He is hurled to the ground and kicked repeatedly...until the angel of death appears to take him home.

Here, in this version of the Roman Coliseum, the ritual is about to begin.

I feel a strong impulse to turn around. I do that, very slowly, and look into eyes of rage. It's the student in the yellow pants.

"*C'mon*," he says, "*c'mon, m———r!*"

Meaning: *Take a swing, and when you miss—they always miss, because they're so scared—we'll get you on the ground....*

◊

It's an act of Providence for which I will always remain grateful.

Two policemen patrolling the area turn a corner and catch sight of the scene. A slight opening in the crowd is just wide enough for them to see three whites, surrounded. Knowing what encirclement means, they rush toward us with pistols ready to fire.

A student shrieks, "*THE POLICE!*"

When one of the patrolman fires into the air, some in the crowd think bullets are aimed at *them*.

Children and some women become hysterical. Sinews are rushing in different directions, to hide somewhere, *anywhere*.

Within minutes, all have vanished, leaving behind a tense hush and a slight breeze passing through empty space.

A policeman comes to me, "You all right?"

"I don't know. Maybe. Barely."

"I understand."

◊

The Brothers who stayed in the car are in shock. After retrieving his backpack, we take the student home.

We return to school in silence. When we arrive, the Brothers are in the middle of a pleasant cocktail social in their residence. Through an open window, you hear loud conversation and laughter.

Kevin looks at me for a long moment, then disappears into the residence.

I walk toward the school. It's Friday, so nobody is in the faculty lounge. I collapse onto a sofa and close my eyes. Darkness drops over me. Images leap through my mind, one after another: the boy in the yellow pants, Kevin, the roar of the crowd, the police, the student telling us he left his bag *back there*, the officer asking, "*You all right?*" And, curiously, an image of a great shade tree.

The clock strikes six.

I lean forward and rest my head on my hands.

After I don't know how long, two words emerge from someplace inside me. I whisper into the dark:

Thank You.

CHAPTER 6

The Slave Cemetery

When you do things from your soul,
you feel a river moving in you, a joy.

When actions come from another section,
the feeling disappears.

—Rumi

My eyelids are starting to feel heavy when I notice a sign on the side of the highway: *Plantation Inn, one mile ahead.* I slow down and turn into a driveway leading to an old southern mansion. As I enter, a young woman smiles from behind the reception desk.

"Welcome! I'm Cynthia Demisse."

After a few minutes of small talk, she asks how long I would like to stay.

"I'm not sure. I'll tell you tomorrow."

Around eleven the next morning, I ask Miss Demisse if the name "Plantation Inn" means that in the past this had been a plantation.

"Yes. They used to grow cotton on big wide fields."

They?

Wherever you had plantations, you were likely to find slaves; and where you had slaves, you had "masters." Many of them were the image and likeness of the ancient Roman *paterfamilias*: the male who governed a household. His wife, children, and slaves were considered property. He could abuse them in any way, and not be prosecuted. The master was free to kill them, if such was his fancy.

It was said of one particular slave owner that in his presence, trees no longer rustled and rabbits stopped squealing on withered grass: both terrified, one no less than the other.

"*Where is the slave cemetery?*"

Miss Demisse runs a hand through her hair.

"How do you know there is a slave cemetery?"

"Trust me, I know. May I visit it?"

Her voice drops low.

"Why would you want to go there?"

"I want to pray at the cemetery."

Nobody is around, so she invites me to sit with her on a sofa.

"This may sound intrusive," she says, gently, "but I can't help it. Please tell me why you are so eager to go to the cemetery."

I feel at ease with Miss Demisse. After a few minutes— although with some awkwardness—I start to share what is so personal. I edge into the story about the little house, and the afternoon I was almost killed.

Twice Miss Demisse says, "*Oh my God.*"

Eventually, she tells me, "The cemetery is deep in the woods. *Very* deep. It's one thing to give directions, and another for you to find it. You could easily get lost. *Easily*. If you do, it's *trouble*."

She gives me the directions, "as best I can."

"I'll pray for you," she says.

Then, on second thought, "No, I'll pray *with* you."

In the afternoon, I start the expedition, hands in pockets. It's around two.

Inside the woods, I roam through bark and mud. Its citizens notice the stranger who has appeared, uninvited. *Who is he? Why is he here? Can he be trusted?*

A buck stares from a clearing, its antlers held high; a cottonmouth catches sight of me. No matter. The distance between us is long enough. We both breathe easily, since neither of us makes a difference to the other.

Starting to dive, a mother hawk changes course when she catches sight of "the stranger." Startled by my footsteps, a brown owl starts to hoot: *Are you here to harm?*

Midway through the second hour, amid the smell of dead leaves, I start to feel uneasy. Am I concerned that I may be lost?

Four o'clock. Something is clicking in the branches of a fig tree. A vision startles me. Ahead in the distance someone is leaning on a fence. He seems to be waiting...*for me.*

But when I draw near, I see no one. My uneasiness shifts into a chill of fear, but only gradually, like a child waking up in bits. I start to sing Frank Sinatra's *New York, New York.* Keep on singing, I tell myself. Remember the time you heard that song in Yankee Stadium?

After two more miles, I remember, "Miss Demisse is praying *with* me."

Less than a mile later, I hold still and stare.

It stares back at me.

The slave cemetery.

Twigs, ragged branches, a dead pine tree, a holly thicket—guards of honor near the graves, not far from a waterfall stream.

A deep hush: the kind that cuts deep into you.

I inch toward the graves. Stones have been jammed into the earth at the head of each one. They bear no name, no date of birth.

Big stones, little stones, tiny stones.

Apparently adults have been buried beneath the big ones. The tiny ones say that it has to be the skeleton of an infant or baby. And the small ones? The remains of children.

I stand in front of a grave guarded by a small stone. My fantasy says it is a small girl. I imagine a conversation:

"My child, please tell me how old you were when you died."

Instead of giving me a date, she makes brief mention of the slow death of her childhood.

I ask, "Who put the stone over your grave?"

She shakes her head.

"Were you captured in Africa? Were you in the hull of a slave ship? Were you torn away from your family at the slave market?"

Silence, only silence.

"Do the questions weary you? Or is your silence a protest against me? After all, I am white."

She assures me that it isn't that. The child changes the subject. She talks about life in her heavenly homeland. It's so beautiful! "Someday you'll see."

I kneel to honor the memory of so many ascended souls, shining bright in the likeness of God's loving kindness. I sense that they are encouraging me to keep moving ahead on my odyssey.

I hum a Negro spiritual over a tiny grave:

No more auction blocks for me,
No more, no more,
No more auction blocks for me,
Many thousand gone...

No more driver's lash for me,
No more, no more.
No more driver's lash for me,
Many thousand gone.*

Christ is at my side. I sense that he was on this land—as a slave—a century ago.

I finish humming the spiritual and pause. When I start again, our voices thread together.

No more driver's lash for me,
No more, no more.
No more driver's lash for me,
Many thousand gone.

Christ is humming, reliving his agony of lash after lash.

---

* Gustavus D. Pike, *The Jubilee Singers* (Boston: Lee and Shepard, 1873), 186, and quoted in Eileen Southern, *The Music of Black Americans. A History*, 2nd ed. (New York: Norton, 1983), 160–61.

CHAPTER 7

The Grand Silence

How much I long for the night to come again—
I am restless all afternoon...
How much I long for the huge stars to appear all
over the heavens,
And the black spaces between those stars....
　　　　—from "Waiting for the Stars" by Robert Bly

They don't just turn up by chance.

It's all part of a ritual started who knows when.

Each night, well before four, what Rilke calls "animals created by silence" start their solemn procession out of the woods,
toward the monastic church.

Coyotes.

They move slowly, careful not to disturb the silence.

By 3:50 a.m., they have assembled, like Benedictine monks
holding still, waiting to process into church for Vespers—two by
two, the abbot leading the way.

At 4:00 a.m., the bells ring. Adrenaline pumps through the
coyotes and they begin to howl. They make such fierce sounds!
When the bells stop ringing, the bodies made of silence process
back to the woods.

Years ago, the great southern writer Flannery O'Connor willed her peacocks to the monastery. The monks built a home for them: a fenced-in area beside a lake. It faced the church. Immediately, the peacocks added their shrill voices to the nightly ritual.

God might have been pleased.

But guests trying to sleep—and the neighbors?

Some may think that nothing much happens at night. They may tolerate the shadows and take the darkness to be an in-between time until the day arrives.

But in the monastery, much happens in the dark during the twelve hours that follow the final communal prayer service of the day. It is a time for monks to go inward, to their Narnia within Narnia, a no-place as vast as the black spaces between the stars.

Even eye contact is avoided, unless there be an emergency.

This sacred time is called *The Grand Silence*: a space for pondering; for prayer; for growing deeper in self-knowledge, kindness, and compassion; and for the ones drawn into the vastness of Narnia within Narnia, a time for closing the eyes and sitting with not a single movement of the body—the stillness symbolizing oneness with God.

Since body and mind go hand in hand, when the mind notices that the body is not moving around, it also slides into stillness.

You never know what time the Brothers will awaken: perhaps one at midnight, another at two, still others at three or three-thirty.

By 3:50, the last of the monks are gliding past each other in the shadows of the cloister, on their way to an immense replica of a twelfth-century monastic church, where Jesus and his Mother are waiting.

Inside the church, a Brother dips his fingers in holy water. Then Christ blesses him through those fingers.

The monk turns toward the sanctuary. He makes a profound bow to Christ, who welcomes him from within the tabernacle that contains his localized presence.

Rising slowly from his bow, the monk walks—not too fast and not too slow—to his place in one of the double lines of choir stalls: the first cluster on the left; the second on the right.

Most with eyes closed, the monks stand in a row, facing the tabernacle.

At four, a bell rings: once, twice, three times…then a pause followed by another three rings and still another pause; then three more rings. *The Angelus.* As the sound of the final ring fades away, a monk chants into the ensuing silence, "*O Lord, open my lips…*"

His Brothers finish the sentence: "*And my mouth shall declare your praise.*"

During Vigils, monks praise and thank God present in the hearts of their Brothers across the way; men whose souls are awake even when the body might feel heavy and sleepy, and the landscape of the mind little more than a blur.

However, at least in some cases, Christ's gentle silence has turned the space inside them into a festival of Light!

Vigils has two parts. After part one, the monks find a spot to pray, ponder, remember, perhaps wrestle on the inside.

One monk says, of an experience at the midpoint period, "The strangest thing happened. After the first part of Vigils, I went to a corner and sat to meditate. Suddenly the bell rang. Monks started to walk back to their choir stalls. I had absolutely no sense of thirty minutes passing by!"

When he asks me about this, I say, "*When you go into a place that is no-place—devoid of time, space, or form—don't be surprised if the bell rings right after you sit down!*"

When voices have ceased chanting, the night speaks of a visual silence, a profound listening, perhaps even the kind of intimacy with God called the gift of contemplative union.

On this particular night, the Grand Silence returns me to *that afternoon*. I remember the next morning, when Br. Kevin said, "*Do you realize what almost happened?*"

Once again, I hear the crowd shrieking, "*Kill them, kill them!*" I relive the impulse to turn around slowly, to look into eyes of rage: a teenager, dressed in pants yellow as dead leaves.

At unexpected times, his eyes haunt me. I imagine my hand shading his eyelids, whispering gently, "*Who did you see when you saw me that afternoon?*"

Was it to the memory of Selma in the evening news, of a white policeman beating a black man with a wrinkled face? Or the vision of a ten-year-old "colored" child, who, after seeing his brother lynched, went mad? Or....

Time will pass, and then... once again, an image of his eyes....

And the usual questions: Is he alive? If so, what is he doing? Has he dealt with his rage? Where is he, spiritually and emotionally?

I keep praying for him. I feel that a bond keeps linking us together.

I tell a friend about this. He doesn't understand, *"The man wanted to kill you!"*

"I know, I know."

◊

"Come to me, all you that are weary and are carrying heavy burdens....for I am gentle and humble in heart" (Matt 11:28–29).

Christ opens a palm, and I plant three thorns on it. They represent the burdens the former student in the yellow pants may be carrying somewhere: brittle, from anguish and pain.

◊

That event has helped me to seal a psalm into the deepest part of my soul. Monks chant it by memory in the dark, in the heart of winter:

You who live in the shelter of the Most High,
who abide in the shadow of the Almighty,
will say to the LORD, "My refuge and my fortress;
my God, in whom I trust." (Ps 91:1–2)

The image of a great shade tree arises from deep unconscious layers, and once again joins the scenes of that dark afternoon.

◊

This psalm is God's gift to each of us. It belongs to you, dear reader, and to my brother, Kevin; and to the crowd that encircled us, and to the student who retrieved his book bag, and to the policemen who saved us.

But in a special and powerful way, it belongs to you, whose name I will never know. The psalm is yours. Receive it, my brother in the yellow pants, and breathe deep beneath the shade of the Most High.

CHAPTER 8

Under a Bridge in South Carolina

I had no idea what life was—
suddenly it was nothing but year after year,
not good anymore, not fresh anymore…
as if torn in two pieces down the center.
                                    —Rainer Maria Rilke

It is 3:00 a.m. inside a monastic guesthouse.

I knock on the door of Fergus Jenkins, a guest I have befriended. Twenty minutes later we are walking through shadows past a bullpen: huge bodies, restless even at this hour. I wonder which of them burst through the boredom of the night, and broke into the barn while the Sisters were milking cows? Nuns wrenched back from the bull, and stabbed at spaces that lead to an exit.

◊

A clearing. Ahead of us is the monastic church silhouetted against the sky, under a full moon. The desert fathers would have called it a "festive hall": a house of prayer where Sisters and guests dance the dance of No One. This takes place in a night-space where nobody is "one"—in the sense of an individual "one" pitted against other individual "ones." It wards off gaps.

◊

Fergus is still trying to make sense of the place. For him, more is guessed than known.

Yesterday, he leaned forward as I described a symposium held at Mount Saviour Monastery in upstate New York years ago. Hindus, Christians, Buddhists, and Muslims attended. It was an assembly of No One, with no religion competing against the others. Fergus liked that.

This is how it ended.

The final words of the symposium spoken, the participants leave the lecture hall for the chapel. They pass between two lines: their hosts, the monks. The passage is a ritual of mutual reverence, of *Namaste*, carried out in silence.

They enter the chapel. The altar is in the middle; everything converges on that focal point, a rock that shimmers. Four double doors open, each one facing a different corner of the universe. A monk rings a bell slowly, solemnly. Its deep sound floats over a nearby forest, where an outlaw preacher has carved something in the tiny burr of a bark. The bell's vibration expands further, halting to hover over a strip mall in the city, to protect an orphan child who has wandered away from her parents.

Everyone leaves through a different door.

Like Mount Saviour, the altar is the axis of this place of festive innocence. The sacred hands of the One glowing inside the tabernacle reach out to touch each visitor, every stranger—and turn him into a friend, no stranger. The Secret One does not recognize distinctions: guests with shoes, guests without shoes, religious, irreligious….No fingerprints, no badges. Everyone is equal, in line with Christ's paradigm of radical equality and inclusivity.

The road to this Cistercian church has been a long and painful one for Fergus. He reminds me of a man I've been reading about in Elie Wiesel's *The Gates of the Forest*: Gregor, a survivor of a death camp. Midway through the book, he challenges a rabbi, "After Auschwitz, how can you still believe in God?"

"After Auschwitz, how can you *not* believe in God?"

Later, Gregor, now conscious of the tears that have gathered in his chest over the years, returns to the hasidic master.

"Rabbi," Gregor pleads, "make me able to weep."

"Not enough," the Rabbi says, "Tears are not enough. I will teach you how to sing."

A young nun whispers into Fergus's ear, "Please come with me to the back of the church."

He looks at me with an almost pleading *what-is-this-all-about* look. I shrug my shoulders. "I don't know."

He rises and follows her.

"You are Fergus?"

"Yes."

The nun identifies herself as Sister Ekaterina. She asks, "Why are you here?"

Her voice is gentle.

"*Do you want me to leave?*"

"Of course not."

"Well then..."

"What have you been thinking about, Fergus?"

He looks away for a moment, wondering if he should answer what he feels is an invasive question from a stranger.

But he does answer, "This place, its silence and its simplicity...its kindness. It makes sense. I'm thinking about the nuns, too. They—you—seem so gentle, genuine, caring. And yet I feel that I'm intruding. If you knew who I was, and what I have been, you would not be speaking with me."

"Why?"

"*Why?* Because for almost three years, I have been living under a bridge in South Carolina. Before that I was an actor. I made it to Broadway three times. But the whole scene made no sense to me. I got more and more lonely and depressed. Some nights, I went sleepless. No one could help me because I wouldn't let anyone into my world. I craved time away from everything and everyone. So I went to South Carolina and became…"

Fergus can't get the words out. To him, they are too shameful.

After a long pause, Sister Ekaterina says, "You went to South Carolina and became…*a street person?*"

"Yes. A street person. *There, I said it.* A street person. I lived—survived—under a bridge. I stayed there, trapped in a kind of bank of fog, until two men appeared one afternoon under the bridge. They said that they had been sent to find me."

"*Sent?* Why? And by whom?"

"They said, 'You've chewed at your lip long enough. This isn't your tribe. You're coming with us.' So they yanked me out of my cage and brought me here…and then disappeared."

"Fergus, were they street people?"

"No. They were strangers. The atmosphere changed under the bridge when they appeared. It was kind of eerie, like the feeling of a wind as a hurricane approaches."

Sister Ekaterina tries to make sense of what has been said.

"Fergus, listen to me. You were a street person, and that's OK, it really is. But now you are a pilgrim. A friend of God."

"What do you mean, *pilgrim?* Something religious?"

"Stick around a while. You'll catch on."

"You listen well—you, of all people, a nun! I would never have dreamed that a nun would listen to me—with respect. I used to be a Catholic. In grade school, the nuns never listened to me. But I don't see you standing with folded arms, obsessed with judging me. I'm curious about you."

"Curiosity is not enough, Fergus. To be inquisitive is not enough, nor are the scattered fragments of your life. I must teach you how to sing!"

A bell tinkles down a long corridor far away. Its sound draws closer.

The nuns rise up from the shadows, take their places in the choir stalls, and face the altar and its tabernacle. The lights—soft and gentle—go on.

Lauds, the Hour of Praise, begins.

The nuns bow, stand, sing, sit—and listen, waiting for *dabar* to sink into their hearts. Then they stand again with grateful faces, and chant—slowly, to a deep rhythm of psalmody—and sing and bow again.

One rhythm, one song: all flowing together inside the Love Canticle of the Great Round Dance.

Lauds concludes.

All the lights go off, except for the one shining over the altar. The old chaplain carries the Blessed Sacrament from the silence of the tabernacle and places it in a vessel on the altar. It will stay there for half an hour.

You see the Eucharistic Presence on top of the wooden altar—and everyone else, encircling that Host like so many spokes of a wheel: Fergus, the chaplain, the bull, the cows, the barn, Ekaterina, and her Sisters.

Dawn.
The eucharistic celebration begins.

From within the Great Round Dance, the Heavenly Father reaches out to everyone. The surface of Christ-water sparkles into wave after wave of endless kindness, coursing back to the silence of the Source of creation.

Rejoicing, he embraces the Son in the "We" of the Blessed Spirit: the strong Wind that hovered on that first day of creation.

Now we receive the Father's love on this eucharistic tide, all from within the Center of the Universe, radiating from the top of that tiny altar cloth.

A climate of *eucharistia*—gratitude—pervades the festive hall and expands beyond the windows of its sacred precincts.

Silence, peace. The sound of mourning doves in the treetops.

The Liturgy has ended.

We are No One.

Thirty minutes after the end of Mass, a door opens. A smiling nun glides into the hall and tells us, in sign language, that we must go outside for a while. She has to clean the church.

Suddenly, I wake up from a heavy sleep and a heavy dream, my book still open at the passage where Odysseus rescues his friends, by giving his name as *No One*.

CHAPTER 9

Gone, Yet Not Away

> May the Son of God, already formed in you, grow to
> the point of becoming immense in you. He will then
> be for you laughter, gladness, and the fullness of joy
> that no one can take from you.
>
> —Isaac of Stella, twelfth-century monk

In our imagination, we may see a beloved who has gone away,
perhaps to another country or to the land beyond all lands. We
may remember the deep-set eyes, the smooth and tender skin,
the tilt of the head, the look on her face after receiving a
lagniappe.

Though not physically present, our beloved may be with us
through reverie, by way of imagination—a person seen, or
touched, as clearly as in the most vivid of dreams.

While in a concentration camp, Viktor Frankl experienced
this kind of presence each time he remembered his wife, his
enchanted princess. Her image was with him at all times. She
shared in his gentle mourning.

Frankl would converse with her: Well, what shall we do
today? What time do you want to see the dentist? Our son,
Michael, how did he do in the play? But now brace yourself for
this. Let me tell you what happened last night—the savage
sounds, the beating of an innocent child....I need you so much,
my beloved.

Viktor Frankl survived the camp. His connection with his wife saved him: proof that *an effective, life-giving presence need not be palpable.*

Not long ago, a young widower asked to speak with a monk. They found me.

When I first saw him, I wondered, *When was the last time that this man slept?*

Jim mentioned his restless nights, and how impossible it had been for him to pray. Everything had changed since his wife died ten months ago.

"Prayer is so dry and meaningless," he said, "and such a waste of time."

I asked him if he believed that Christ is in our neighbor; that Christ *is* our neighbor.

It took Jim a long time to reply, "Yes."

"Do you believe that your wife is Jesus because she is sharing in his life?"

More awkward silence.

A nervous cough.

With reluctance, "Yes."

"Then why not pray to Christ in her, Jim? To speak with her is to speak with Jesus. You don't know what Christ looked like, but you have no trouble remembering your wife's face, her smile, the way she tipped her head back before reading a poem. In other words, visualize her—as Christ—when you pray."

Jim appeared at the guesthouse five weeks later, looking calm and refreshed, as though he had finally been able to sleep well.

"Two weeks after I left here, I visualized my wife," he said. "She spoke with me, and I with her. *I had a definite sense that she was Christ, here and now.*"

As the widower continued this practice, his prayer life deepened and his grief lessened.

Two of his friends took up the practice, calling to mind and heart the image of the person who had most loved them—without a single condition.

One of them said, "The room was filled with silence the moment I saw her image in my awareness. At that moment, I *knew* that she was Christ..."

"And?"

And....

CHAPTER 10

Another Dream

When you begin to touch your heart or let your
heart be touched, you begin to discover that it's
bottomless...that this heart is huge, vast, and
limitless. You begin to discover how much warmth
and gentleness is there, as well as how much
space....

—Pema Chödrön

Time stands still throughout a dream in which Christ leads me
deep into a forest. The silence is overwhelming. How did we get
here within seconds?

I am young.

Jesus quotes from a Jewish Midrash. It goes this way—
more or less: "Shortly before someone is to leave his earthly existence, the Lord appears to him and says, 'Record all you have
accomplished.' The man does as he is told and sets his seal to all
he has written."

Christ hands me an open notebook. *Does this mean I am
about to die?*

Without asking the question, I sit and write. I put to paper
as much as I can remember of the most significant deeds of my
life, good and bad. I conclude this way, perhaps—or probably—
wanting to present myself in a favorable light, "I've tried to speak
only what is good and true in the few years I've been on this earth.

I'm a raw and fragile—and very impulsive—young man. I've tried my best, but haven't done as good a job as I would have wanted, in being kind to people without expecting a return. I feel really bad about that because I want to love people the way you do."

As I write that, I feel like adding, "I haven't done too well because it's been *all me* trying to do good without looking to you for help." But I don't write that. I'm not sure why.

I hand the notebook back to Christ, who looks at what I have written. He nods and hands it back to me.

"Burn the notebook," he says.

As I sink deeper into my imagination, I find myself in a foreign country. But which one? France? Brazil? Nigeria? India? Turkey? Some other?

Here, everyone speaks a different language, yet communicates with everyone and is understood. *How can that be?*

A man smiles at you? He is your friend for life. A woman offers you a meal? She takes you to her kitchen. She pries oysters open and leaves them to drain, then coats them with breadcrumbs. There, done.

Fried oysters are presented to me at the dining room table, along with green turtle soup and salmon with lobster sauce...and dressed salad and sweetbreads. The hostess makes an observation, with a gentle smile, "For so thin a lad, you do put it away."

A thrill runs through my body. I want to sing and dance. Just as that desire manifests, a wind sweeps me into the sky. I land inside Preservation Hall, in New Orleans's French Quarter. Photos of great musicians decorate the walls: Count Basie, Louie Armstrong, Lester Young....

Christ enters the Hall carrying a platter of triangular pastries. He announces to the hushed crowd that they are for his friend—*me*! He sets the platter on my table, and says that I am not to eat the pastries until after I have danced.

Fulfillment of desire! I leap to my feet and dance, whirling around and around, as only the gypsies of Andalusia can dance...or so I think. The musicians and visitors applaud with gusto. Someone takes up the sax and plays with a kind of intensity I have never experienced.

Invigorated, I return to the table. Christ is sitting alongside Louie Armstrong. My Lord looks at me and says, "This is *brik*, the national food of Tunisia. Louie wants to show us how to eat it."

Centering Prayer

> The fundamental goodness of human nature...is an
> essential element of Christian faith. This basic core
> of goodness is capable of unlimited development,
> indeed, of becoming transformed into Christ and
> deified.
>
> —Thomas Keating

In one of his poems, W. S. Merwin relates evil to kindly members of sewing circles in little towns in Pennsylvania.* We may take "evil" to mean what destroys, dilutes or weakens life. The members of the sewing circle have been good and virtuous, yet unknowingly have lived lives diluted or weakened by a lack of contact with their inmost identity, rooted in God. For the most part, it's through no fault of their own. Rather it's a case of mystification by a social consensus that assumes that nothing goes on beneath the level of thoughts, feeling, images, or memory.

The practice of Centering Prayer helps a person to live from his basic core of goodness. He is capable of being changed into the likeness of God.

Thomas Keating holds that the source of Centering Prayer is the indwelling Trinity. But this sacred source points to a more horizontal origin: the ancient Christian tradition, in particular

---

* W. S. Merwin, "Small Woman on Swallow Street," in *The First Four Books of Poems* (Port Townsend, WA: Copper Canyon Press, 2000), 261.

the experiential teachings of St. John of the Cross and the four-teenth-century spiritual classic, "The Cloud of Unknowing." While deepening trust in God, the practice allows the unfolding of wakeful receptivity and the gradual maturation of consciousness. It refines and prepares the intuitive faculties to receive the sudden, unexpected, and unmerited gift of contemplation.

Each prayer session deepens inner silence. In a skillful way, this practice dismantles what Fr. Thomas Keating identifies as the primary wound of the human condition: the illusion that God is absent.

Centering Prayer affirms the experiential reality of a vast, silent, and gentle Presence in which—whether we are aware of it or not—at every moment, we "live and move and have our being." Through practice, one slowly evolves into the happiness that, Fr. Keating says, "can be found only in the experience of union with God, the experience that also unites us to everyone else in the human family and to all reality."*

Some practical instructions follow:

1. Before beginning the practice of Centering Prayer, choose a sacred word to represent your intention to yield to the divine presence and action operating from the inmost level of soul: the "second heart" to which only God has access. The sacred word might be a name of God, or some word with which you feel comfortable—such as *love, peace, silence, joy, stillness.* The word may be no word, but simply the breath.

2. While sitting comfortably with eyes closed, introduce the sacred word at the quietest level of inner speech, almost a whisper. Your intention renewed,

---

* Thomas Keating, *The Mystery of Christ: The Liturgy as Spiritual Experience* (New York: Continuum, 1994), 5.

it then becomes a matter of alert receptivity: of being, and not doing; of expectant waiting, accompanied by persistent energy.

3. Within this context, "thoughts" may be more than ideas, reflections, or commentaries. They may include sensations, images, plans, and spiritual communications. When your attention strays into a thought or series of thoughts, gently allow the sacred word to whisper itself within you. Each time this is done, you reaffirm your intention to remain open to God's presence and action.

4. When the practice ends, remain in silence for two minutes with eyes closed. For Thomas Keating, "this gives the psyche a brief space to readjust to the external senses, and a better chance of bringing the atmosphere of interior prayer into the activities of daily life."*

---

* Thomas Keating, "Centering Prayer," in Michael Downey, *The New Dictionary of Catholic Spirituality* (Collegeville, MN: The Liturgical Press, 1993), 139.

A Journey Waiting to Begin

Pilgrims are persons in motion—seeking something we might call completion.

—Richard R. Neibuhr

CHAPTER 1

Into the Land of Likeness

God created a reminder, an image.
Humanity is a reminder of God.
As God is compassionate,
Let humanity be compassionate.

—Abraham Heschel

Christ's fundamental paradigm of radical equality and inclusivity shone brightly from the beginning of time. God created all human beings with an identical share of his image. We are born blessed with *inherent nobility*—a term which has nothing to do with aristocracy. It means inner luminosity, a brightness that radiates from within our inner spaciousness.

Christ emphasizes our nobility when he says, "*You are the light of the world.*"

Perhaps Jesus is saying, "You are the image of our Heavenly Father; a portrait of his limitless goodness, a replica that is home to his characteristics."

These qualities reflect a different side of God's *hesed*, a Hebrew word translated as "mercy, or unconditional kindness and unrestricted compassion."

God created us so that, each in our unique way, we might mirror Divine Mercy by gradually becoming *kindness incarnate*.

This is the goal, or life purpose, of every human being.

We are drawn out of nothingness into a body and soul that have at their center the image of God. The ancient Cistercian monks spoke of the long journey out of the land of unlikeness (nothing of the qualities of God being lived out) to a gradual movement into and through the land of likeness: the process of gradually unfolding what has always been inside us—the various qualities of God, present in his image: silence, gentleness, kindness, compassion, deep listening, gentle strength, and humility.

Is God *humble*?

Humble derives from the Latin *humus*, "earth." To be humble is to be earthed in reality. God is grounded in what truly is, at an infinite level of truth. Because humility is part of the divine image, when we grow in that value increasingly, we reflect God's humility. We see things as they are, from within the vastness of our Creator.

This gradual transformation from image to likeness manifests in the fruits of the Spirit. A consistent living of these fruits is known as "spontaneous right action." When this kind of action becomes second nature, we are living out of the spaciousness deep within us, where we are one with God.

The scenario is well-known: Jesus tracing something on the earth slowly and meticulously.

We don't know what he drew, but we recognize the effect: something "exploded" inside the rough and violent men who were so eager to stone a woman to death. One by one they dropped their stones and shuffled away.

The poet Tomas Tranströmer depicts a man in an open field alone, tracing something on the earth.

Elsewhere, he finds a cross hanging in a cool church vault. Tranströmer senses the power in its four beams. They explode into the universe: north, south, east, and west. At times, the cross resembles "a split-second shot of something rushing forward at tremendous speed."*

But doesn't something like that—at least on occasion— happen to a person who has slept for a long time, spiritually and/or emotionally? She awakens, "catches sight" of the image of God radiating inside her, and at that moment, a longing to evolve into the divine likeness bounds into life!

She is in the center of the cross, her breath in tune with the Spirit's breath, both rushing ahead at immense speed toward a journey waiting to begin.

Whether we know it or not, we long to grow beyond what the writer, Sharon Salzberg, calls *the randomness of sheer happenings.*† We yearn to create and receive meaning by drawing daily events and circumstances into a flexible thread.

This thread tends to become increasingly stable when we embark on a *spiritual journey with a purpose.* Then we interact with all that is, through the lens of that unifying goal. This journey is an *odyssey*: a term that most dictionaries would define as "a daring undertaking" that involves a willingness to take chances and a determination to evolve.

According to the ancient Hebrew tradition, on the Sabbath, God creates an extra soul, which empowers us to fully honor and

---

* Tomas Transtrÿmer, "Out in the Open" ("I Det Fria"), in Robert Hass, ed., *Tomas Transtrÿmer: Selected Poems 1954–1986*, trans. Robert Bly (Hopewell, NJ: The Eco Press, 1987), 87.

† Sharon Salzberg, *Faith: Trusting Your Own Deepest Experience* (New York: Riverhead Books, 2002), 23.

appreciate ourselves and others, especially the people God has sent into our lives. Then we love our neighbors as ourselves.

But this extra soul does not appear *only* on the Sabbath. It is an essential part of our humanity.

The Jungian analyst Robert Johnson finds that people resist the noble aspects of their lives more forcefully than they hide their dark sides. As he puts it, "It is more disrupting to find that you have a profound nobility of character than to find out that you are a bum."

When the Dalai Lama met with educators during an American tour, he asked, "What is the greatest obstacle to the inner evolution of your students?"

Many answered, "self-hatred."

Self-hatred? The Dalai Lama didn't understand the word.

His interpreter drew him aside to explain what the term meant since *self-hatred* does not exist in the Tibetan culture. After fifteen minutes, the interpreter carried a message to the educators, "The Dalai Lama is in shock. He cannot understand how anyone could hate the radiance that shines in all of us."

When beauty is there to be touched, why do more than a few look at themselves and others through a lens of unworthiness and judgment? Ask the breakers that roar inside the deep waters of the mind. These afflictive thoughts convinced the writer Henri Nouwen that he was unloved.

Have you read *Genesee Diary*, Nouwen's account of his sabbatical at a Trappist monastery? In it, the abbot points out that when Nouwen's mind interprets someone's attitude as a rejection, he feels totally unloved. This leads to something of a blind rage.

"I keep hoping for a moment of full acceptance," Nouwen writes, "a hope I attach to every little event. A small rejection easily leads to devastating despair and a feeling of total failure."*

To help him internalize the meaning of "full acceptance by God," the abbot suggests that he take as his mantra "*I am the glory of God.*"

Merriam-Webster defines *glory* as "great beauty and splendor."

Eventually, Nouwen moves closer to internalizing the words of the twelfth-century monk William of St. Thierry: *O image of God, recognize your dignity; let the effigy of your creator shine forth in you.…To yourself you seem of little worth, but in reality you are precious.*

◊

In the fourth century, the great desert father Anthony said, "The one who loves and honors himself, loves and honors all."

Monks of the Cistercian "Golden Age" of the twelfth century, such as William of St. Thierry, Aelred of Rievaulx, John of Forde, and Gilbert of Hoyland, echoed this conviction. They taught that the only way to fulfill the purpose of creation was to accept and revere others, *as well as oneself*. These monks did not confuse self-respect with selfishness or conceit. Long before the findings of contemporary psychology, they realized that, without appropriate self-care, they would not be of much help to their brothers, or to the strangers who came to them for a word from God. These ancients knew from experience that self-respect and appropriate self-care would keep them from running out of things to give…with compassion, and a gentleness born of the quiet ways of the Great Blue Heron.

---

* Henri J. M. Nouwen, *The Genesee Diary* (New York: Doubleday/Image, 1981), 52.

CHAPTER 2

A Yearning to Unfold

I want to unfold. I don't want to stay folded
anywhere, because when I am folded, there I am
untrue.

—Rainer Maria Rilke

From the moment God created us, we breathed in tune with His
sacred breath, in the long spring of eternity.

The word *spirit* derives from the Latin *spiritus*, "breath."
The Holy Spirit is God's Breath: a titanic potency that inserts
time, space, and form into its Immensity.

The fourth century Christian monk Ammonas was heard to
say, "God breathes, and we breathe the breath of God." The Spirit
guides us on the long journey from image to likeness.

Whenever we have any experience at all, we may accurately depict it by saying that, at that moment, we are conscious
of something. The object of experience may be concrete (e.g., a
table), more abstract (e.g., a thought), or illusory (e.g., a dream).

But the Spirit can never be an object of perception because
we are *inside* God's vastness. We are not aware *of* that spaciousness. We simply live in God.

Now, this is how I understand it.

So that the divine image might unfold into likeness in creating us, God implants the power of desire at the inmost level of consciousness: a longing to unfold, to blend into God.

○

Healthy desire invites us to bring forth the goodness in other people, as well as in ourselves.

But if desire is misdirected, the result is entanglement in what the Arab tradition calls the *nafs*: the bitter, folded soul of the greedy one, driven by its eating energy.

The first emperor of China wanted to "eat the whole world."

The *nafs* tries to dismantle whatever stands in the way of its compulsion to "eat" power, prestige, the approval of others, money, the feeling that "I am the center of the universe," and ambition. The virulent pride of the *nafs* longs to dominate and devour the autonomy of human beings and to blur any impression of God *as he really is*.

○

God implants a second piece to help in the unfolding of the divine image: *a dynamic, evolutionary impulse* that would turn yearning into a process of growing into the likeness of God and actualizing our permanent identity, rooted in God.

Gradually, we are changed into his likeness, as Christ's gentle kindness loosens one finger after another of a fist that grasps the image. As the fingers are loosened, gradually we come to listen and love as Christ does: gently, without fuss, in a marvel of beauty.

○

In various ways, the ancient Christian sages say the same thing: *God became human so that humans might become God*. The

Greek Fathers call this process *divinization*: an ever-deepening participation in divine life. St. Maximus the Confessor offers an image to explain the process of transformation. He asks us to imagine what happens if we plunge iron into fire. The flames penetrate the metal, communicating some of its properties to the iron. The metal becomes hot and malleable. It starts to glow.

Iron is firm, inflexible, cold, and dense, but when it participates in the nature of the fire, it takes on the qualities of the flames, and yet remains iron. The flames penetrate the metal, communicating some of its properties. God penetrates our humanity, sharing his characteristics.

The iron partakes in the nature of the fire while remaining metal. We share God's nature while remaining our unique selves.

Before it all started, God instilled in each soul the vocation to participate in his nature: to be changed from the potential of the divine image to its gradual actualization, to the point of becoming kindness—and silence—incarnate.

God offers this message to each of us through the lips of the prophet Isaiah: "You were in my care even *before you were born*" (44:2 CEV).

Many years later, God speaks to us through St. Paul: "*Before the first day of creation*, I called you into existence so that you might be holy, blameless, filled with kindness and compassion..." (Eph 1:4, au. trans.).

God first blesses us in *no-time*. Then he brings us—and a spark of infinity in our inmost self—into the land of time...and changes us gradually into the likeness of the Great Heart.

We become human so that Christ's incarnation might continue through our own, for the benefit of all human beings, and for the unfolding of the unique selves that we are.

CHAPTER 3

Honoring Our Uniqueness

When we ask, "Am I following a path with heart?"
we discover that no one can define for us exactly
what our path should be. Instead, we must allow the
mystery and beauty of this question to resonate
within our being.

—Jack Kornfield

In 135 BCE, the Roman Emperor, Hadrian, ordered his henchman, Rufus, to torture Rabbi Akiva for helping his people to
understand the Scriptures. He was eighty-five.

As Rufus separates the rabbi's skin from his bones, Akiva is
praying the *Shema*, since it is the time of day to recite it. According
to Annie Dillard, Rufus is spooked when the dwindling rabbi continues to pray throughout his agony. The henchman asks him—
"conversationally," Dillard adds—if he is a sorcerer.*

Akiva shakes his head slowly, from side to side.

After his grim ordeal ends, Akiva's disciples carry him off to
die. Akiva shocks everyone when he announces that he is a failure. His rabbi asks why he feels that way.

"Because I have not lived like Moses."

Akiva starts to weep, "I am afraid of God's judgment!"

---

* Annie Dillard, *For the Time Being* (New York: Alfred A. Knopf, Inc., 1999), 29.

His rabbi leans toward the frightened man's ear and whispers gently, "*God will not judge Akiva for not being Moses. He will rejoice because Akiva was Akiva.*"

Transformation unfolds within the context of an evermaturing humanity; one that moves gradually toward deeper levels of likeness in an original way. As our odyssey unfolds, increasingly we listen and love—with gentleness—as Christ does, but in a way unlike anyone else. None of us is the same, and we like it that way.

This means that comparisons are not only useless, but they are obstacles to continuing the transformative process. If I say, "I am better than them," I am falling into pride. If the line is "Compared to them, I am a worm," I am doing harm to myself by not honoring my inherent nobility. I may have *done* something wrong, but I *am* not wrong.

Abraham Heschel contends that every human being has something to say, to think, or to do that is unprecedented. This will also happen in the world to come, where Akiva is still Akiva, enjoying every moment of his uniqueness.

CHAPTER 4

The Prez

In America kings or dukes or counts don't amount
to much. But the president does. So I started to call
Lester President. It got shortened to "Prez."
                                        —Billie Holiday

To say that Lester Young was unique is far more than an understatement. I learned about him when I was young through Bill Milkowski's book *Swing It!*

The author describes an idiosyncratic musician who consumes buttermilk and whiskey, or sardines with ice cream. Lester never says "you failed," but rather, "you were bruised." Nor would he ask, "Can your wife cook?" but instead, "Can madam burn?" Whether male or female, Lester Young called everyone "lady."

Billie Holiday claims that Lester is the president, or *The Prez*, of tenor saxophonists. To which no musician takes exception.

◊

The Prez refuses to allow alien eyes to dictate his identity and self-worth. He trusts himself and owns and honors his inherent goodness. He chooses to live from within outwards.

In many ways, he resembles Rosa Parks.

Back in the days of "colored only" signs, when Rosa is asked why she has chosen a seat in the white section of a bus, she replies, "Because I am tired."

Rosa Parks is tired of being abused, subjected to a violence that threatens to take away her soul and to hammer her humanity into subhuman form. Rosa Parks is exhausted from having to defend herself against attempts to force her to relinquish her inner truth. She is tired of having to fight attempts to compel her to believe that she is what certain white folks have decided she must be, and not be. Because of her fierce—and sacred—courage, at no point does Rosa Parks release a defeated scream.

Lester Young and Rosa Parks claim as their own the power of the slaves who refused to be disempowered, as they stood tall and sang spirituals in cotton fields: the sacred music that gave birth to the blues and to jazz.

The blues are about loss, and if the slaves sang them, their song was about the loss of their homeland—but never about the loss of their nobility and inner freedom.

At times, The Prez's idiosyncrasies overshadowed the deeper meaning of some of the seemingly crazy things he did. Prez kept a tiny whiskbroom in his top jacket pocket, to symbolically sweep away insults or anything that might threaten to take away his peace. The broom represented his determination to refuse to hand over his innate nobility to a would-be abuser. He was his own man, firmly grounded in his inner truth.

Growing up, it was only a matter of time before I began to learn the meaning of symbolism and of the importance of living from the inside, and the value of carrying around my version of an invisible tiny whiskbroom in the top pocket of an invisible jacket.

CHAPTER 5

Dream with Both Eyes Open

> I feel as though I'm going to burst, and I know that it would get better with crying, but I can't. I'm restless. I go from one room to the other, breathe through the crack of a closed window....I feel utterly confused, don't know what to read, what to write, what to do. I only know that I am longing.
> —Anne Frank, a Jewish teenager
> hiding from the Nazis

Every human being is blessed with two echoes from beyond. The first is shared by all: to cooperate with the Great Spirit in the unfolding of the divine image into likeness. The second is shared with no one since it is unique, particular, specific—*intended for me only*.

◊

"It is a strange and wondrous place—as monasteries typically are," the writer Paul Wilkes says, "too sensuous and exquisite a setting for a life considered austere, marginal, or irrelevant to that which we know as *the real world*."*

---

* Paul Wilkes, *Beyond the Walls: Monastic Wisdom for Everyday Life* (Chicago: ACTA Publications, 2010), 2.

Wilkes is struggling to discern whether he belongs in a monastery. He pulls a novel, his own, off the shelf. Wilkes opens to a passage that depicts an earnest but conflicted man who has spent months praying and fasting. He is struggling in his discernment.

But after so many women in his life, he has finally met *the one*.

When he starts to talk with her about seeking God's face, she asks him to look into her face instead.

"I'm searching for God's will," he says. "I want to do what God has planned for me."

The woman puts her hands on his cheeks and gazes deeply into his eyes.

"God wants what *you* want," she says.

"Will" is a translation of the Greek *thelema*, which is faithful to the original Aramaic word used by Jesus. *Thelema* means "desire, yearning, longing."

The term *will* is tenacious, disposed to yield not a single inch: "This is my will!"

How different it is to hear God say, "This is what I long for."

Desire, yearning, longing: all these belong to the vocabulary of intimacy.

With the utmost reverence, God sets before each human being various options: marriage, the single life, priesthood, and so much more.

But then he might get more specific: Educator? Hospice worker? Cook? And other possibilities.

The Great Spirit does not hesitate to suggest lifestyles that some find hard to understand, let alone accept: artists, musicians, poets, monks....

◊

Christ assures us that all of these lifestyles are good. "But," he asks, "*which one is good for you? Is this what you really want? Will it benefit others?*"

When God's longing joins our desire, we may begin to speak of "vocation" in a more definitive way.

◊

Desire invites us to open our inmost world to God's Desire. Like Anne Frank, we may be longing—so longing—for him, feeling as if we are going to burst, to break down and weep—but for some reason can't, or won't.

Restless, we may pace from one end of a long corridor to the other, too agitated to close the eyes long enough to pray. But—who knows?—at some unexpected moment, we might be caught off-guard by a gentle, conscious silence: a Presence that yearns for us to let go of all the doing, all the seeking, all the speculating, all the rhetoric.

◊

James talks—or mutters—to himself a lot. The *nafs*? He has never heard the word, but has lived its essence since he was a competitive child. Now the man has nothing left to strive for, no work to serve as the source of his value and identity. He wonders what madness drove him to retire while he was still a highly successful business executive.

James has lived his life in the head. He enjoys reading about theories and ideas—any, but his own. He is a devotee of Ken Wilber. But James doesn't know what to make of Wilber's conviction that "the classic spiritual journey always begins elitist and ends egalitarian. *Always!*"

But he relates well to Wilber's use of the term *always*. Along with *everyone* and *nobody*, *always* is part of his vocabulary. People are *always* gossiping. *Everyone* is narcissistic. *Nobody* listens.

Bored, he walks outside to his garden, and his beloved Spanish moss. A stray thought tells him—*again*—that it has been almost two years since he retired from the corporate world when he should have continued a life of success. The madness of it all! He could return to that world, but something holds him back.

Images of his most important accomplishments start to speed through his inner world. To him, it has *always* been normative to "climb the corporate ladder." Doesn't *everyone* "in the contest" do that? *Nobody* disputes the fact that one must win, at all costs.

At times, he wonders, *did I really win?* The question usually leads to anxiety and, at times, to depression.

James Jerald still does not realize that all his doings have had a single purpose: to grasp the approval of eyes other than his own!

James has been caught off-guard. His mind starts to derail, to swerve out of control in an unfamiliar land inside him, where a thought churns. When he hears it, he starts to feel like a puppy thrashing around in a gunnysack.

When I die, will my achievements cease to exist?

He shouts aloud, "*No, impossible!*"

Then, in a restrained tone of voice, "Surely they will follow me into the next world, where I will be admired as much as I have been lauded in this world…"

A shocking question creeps up on him: What if his accomplishments do *not* follow him into the other world?

The puppy starts to thrash around even more!

If it will not follow me into the next world, then what has been the point of all the toil—and turmoil—that led to a nervous breakdown, a divorce, and the disintegration of my family?

So now what?

Could it be that new life is starting to awaken in James Jerald and that the gunnysack will burst open?

Or will he retreat back into the head and revisit Ken Wilber?

CHAPTER 6

What Have You Done with Your Life?

This world's a city full of straying streets,
And death's the market-place where each one meets.
                                        —Shakespeare

Andalusia. Wherever you go, you hear the same word: in the streets of Cádiz, where lovers walk hand in hand, or in the deep night of Granada, where gypsies gather to fling their ballads into the waters of the Mediterranean.

Duende is an untranslatable word, with several layers of meaning. One of them is "Death is with me on my journey as a fellow pilgrim—every step of the way."

The Spanish poet Federico Garcia Lorca says that outside of his country, when someone dies, they shut the curtains; but in Spain, they open them. It is a country open to death.

Sometimes, rarely, you hear about *duende* outside of Spain. In Germany, Goethe described it once—while talking about Paganini—as a force that everyone feels, but philosophers cannot define.

"The *duende* is not in the throat," an old maestro of the guitar told Lorca. "It climbs up inside you, from the soles of the feet."

"From the soles of the feet": as from the outer self to the depths of the soul.

In most countries, to speak of death is a taboo, or a social blunder. In America, at a seminar on death and dying, a twenty-eight-year-old nurse and mother of four, in the last stages of cancer, asked an audience, "How would you feel if you came into a hospital room to visit a twenty-eight-year-old mother dying of cancer?" The answers: angry, confused, full of horror, full of pity, sad, frustrated. Then the nurse put another question to the group, "Suppose *you* were the twenty-eight-year-old mother dying of cancer. How would you feel if everyone who walked into the room came in with those feelings?"

Within seconds the group realized how much they had surrounded the patient with their own reactions to death and ignored *her*. They saw to what extent they had overlooked the twenty-eight-year-old mother of four, a woman who needed, and deserved, to be understood.

Living *duende* does not mean that we know when—or how—we will die. The nurse did not have to be terminally ill to feel its power.

According to another layer of the word, to live with *duende* means that, following an important turning point, we begin to flow with a greater awareness of context: a continuum of experience that stretches from birth until after death.

This is what makes *duende* and the virtue of hope such friends. They resemble two delicate flowers touching each other lightly. Like *duende*, hope lives in the present moment—and reaches beyond it.

During our lifetime, each of us stitches together our unique story: a biography woven into the broader and vaster fabric of human history—either enhancing or diminishing the quality of the life of that global reality. We carry our history into the other world.

◊

According to Elie Wiesel, legend has it that the Angel of Death is "made up of eyes, only eyes. All he does is look, he kills by looking."

On the contrary, the Angel is not there to kill, but to support—to accompany us into an unfamiliar land.

◊

What happens after we have entered the other world?

For forty years, extensive research has been done on the *near-death experience*, during which persons have been pronounced clinically dead, and are later restored to life. After death, one finds himself in a weightless body of light. It is able to feel, perceive, think, imagine, and remember. Communication is through thought transference.

A common element in the accounts of these subjects is a rendezvous with a "Being of Light," who unseals memories and goes straight to the heart of the matter: *How much have you learned—and loved?*

An interesting question, when we recall that in the Gospels the Great Heart of Jesus emphasizes that kindness, compassion, and forgiveness, expressed as radical equality and inclusivity, are the criteria for "life success." The same criteria accompany the pilgrim as he carries his life history across an open checkpoint into his rendezvous with the Being of Light.

The subject feels accepted, secure, at ease with this Luminous Person, who leaves an impression of indescribable kindness.

◊

Long before research on the near-death experience began, a respected physician, George Ritchie, died of double-lobar pneumonia. Nine minutes later he was revived.

Ritchie recalls staring in astonishment as the brightness of the Being of Light increased. It appeared to shine everywhere at once. The physician felt "an astonishing love" flowing from its radiance.

Ritchie began to step into every episode of his life, in the company of the Light, which surrounded him on all sides. The physician relived all that he had thought, desired, and done, or failed to do—all illuminated by "that searing Light." He had no sense of time passing.

Implicit in each episode was a question that appeared to emerge from the Light: "George, what did you do with your life?"

At a certain point, the doctor got desperate: had he done *anything* that seemed worthwhile? He recalled his greatest moment: becoming an Eagle Scout. But no sooner had he remembered this than he understood that—as at other times in his life—he had stood at the center of the scene: *me, me, ME....*

George Ritchie realized that he, the psychiatrist, was the one discerning the episodes to be selfish or trivial. The Light held him in its gentle embrace. Its question—what have you done with your life?—had nothing to do with accomplishments, or with the myriad ways that Ritchie had devised to impress others.

It was a gentle way of asking, How much have you extended yourself—with no hidden motive—to others, for their good, the way I have to you, without a single reservation? How much have you loved and honored yourself?

From start to finish, these are the questions that all human beings are asked to take seriously. On the one hand, we notice the challenge of gradually relinquishing illusions of grandiosity and the tight grip of self-centeredness; and on the other, the task of accepting ourselves as the warmth of a Secret Friend would have us do.

We come out of the mother naked, with wrinkled skin and sightless eyes. But how we return to the Mother of Silence and Light, the Mother of Love—is another question.

Our pilgrimage is a return to childhood in the gospel sense: a recovery of our "original features," in the image of the Secret One.

Years ago, I read *The Unblinding*, a book of poems by Laurence Lieberman. To become a child in the gospel sense is to "unblind": to see with the eyes of silence, love, and light, in the likeness of God.

And the *duende*?

Another layer of the word suggests that death is the flow from silence and love to deeper silence and greater love. *Duende* is the light that takes us beyond an open checkpoint to a continuation of the "unblinding" begun in this body.

CHAPTER 7

The Last Dance

Pilgrims are persons in motion—seeking something
we might call completion.

—Richard R. Neibuhr

Unusual wasn't the word for him. *Strange?* Not that either.
Different? Perhaps.

The day he arrived at the monastery, the young man looked
so normal: a few drops of rain shining on his eyelashes, dunga-
rees, a backpack tied behind a pinstripe New York Yankee jersey.
His eyes sparkled with unrestrained curiosity.

His features radiated energy, the kind you just wanted to be
around. However, I sensed that if you penetrated beneath the
exterior of a carefree young man, you might discover the husk of
a faraway land you would find hard to identify.

When he passed through the guesthouse entrance the first
day, he strolled over to the reception desk. The monk, who had
been stringing beads to fit a rosary, looked up and greeted his
new guest.

"Welcome, welcome, my good lad. I'm Brother Simon. It's
good to have you with us."

"Thank you, Brother. I'm Inman."

"Ah, so *you're* Inman. Good, good! Now Inman, you forgot
to include your last name when you wrote. May I have it, please?"

"I have none."

Resembling a child, the Brother cups a hand to his mouth, covering a wide smile.

"You don't have a last name? *For real?*"

"For real, Brother. Does it matter?"

"If not to you, then neither to me, but is it legal to have no last name? I mean, for tax purposes and those things?"

Inman shrugs.

"I don't know."

"So Inman, where are you from?"

"I know this will sound more than weird, but I'm from nowhere...*in particular.*"

"From nowhere...in particular?"

"I don't stay put. I'm constantly on the go. I travel a lot. I do what I was sent to do, then leave."

Inman seizes Simon's temporary confusion and retreats into thought as a chance to satisfy his own curiosity, "Brother, how long have you been here?"

Simon edges back into the conversation. He answers, "Sixty years, more or less."

"More or less?"

"You stop counting after a certain point. One of my closest friends, a football player when I was at Notre Dame, wrote to our class last month. He said, '*We're all in the fourth quarter. What we don't know is whether it's the beginning, middle, or end of the quarter.*' Do you know what, Inman? I'm at the far end! It's like traveling toward the ocean on a summer vacation. The closer you get, the more you catch a wee bit of the delightful scent of the water! I may not have arrived in the next world yet, but I sure can sense it."

"Don't be surprised," Inman says, "if you find me at the ocean waiting for you!"

"Oh?"

"Inman, how do you make a living?"

"I don't make a living. *I dance.*"

"You dance?"

"Yes, but not in the way that you might think. What makes it different is...*duende*..."

Inman's voice trails off when he says *duende*.

Br. Simon leans forward: "*Duende*, Inman? What is *that*?"

"Here's an example of *duende*," Inman says. "This would be from the unfortunate occasion when Pastora Pavón sang in a tiny tavern in Andalusia. Federico Garcia Lorca can't get the scene out of his mind. It appears in one of his writings. He recalls that 'her voice of shadow, of beaten tin' drove her audience into a heavy cloud."

"Poor Pastora Pavón," Inman says. "She finishes her song, and nobody applauds. All you get is dense silence. Pastora slumps into a chair, her face flushed. After a minute or so an old man shouts, *Viva Paris!* Meaning *Here skill means nothing!*"

"*That's enough!*" Pastora Pavón leaps to her feet. The reactions of the audience and the old man have awakened the passion of *duende* in her body and soul. She has blended into *Sophia*, the Holy Spirit! Pastora Pavón starts to sing!

"*And how she sang!*" Lorca recalls. "Her voice...opened like a ten-fingered hand...pure music with a body so lean it could stay in the air!"

"Angels sing with *duende*," Inman says. "And yet each one's expression of *duende* differs, depending on what the Creator means for him to do. But all have one thing in common: each one is *malakh*, 'an angel.' But the Hebrew word introduces a second meaning to *malakh*: 'messenger.'"

Inman reminds Br. Simon that Christ had sent angels to deliver the message: *Do not be afraid.*

Two days later, after a long conversation with Inman, the abbot invites the young man to dance in the chapter room following the afternoon prayer service.

"Tomorrow around 2:35. Brother Simon will escort you there. You should have a good turnout—if only out of curiosity. A number of brothers have heard about you!"

The next day, fifty monks gather to watch Inman perform one dance after another, before announcing, "*This will be the last dance.*"

It will be a tribute to Fr. Ludovicus, whom he respects and admires, even though they have never met.

"That will change soon," Inman says, rather casually.

Two monks look at each other, "What does he mean, *that will change soon*? Is he going to Asia, where Ludovicus is attending that monastic conference?"

One of the two, Brother Simon, thinks to himself, "I must ask Inman what he meant by that."

Meticulously, with reverence, Inman pulls on a white cowl: a long flowing garment with wide sleeves that reach down to the ankles—the centuries old garment of the Cistercian monk.

He switches on a tape recorder: a gypsy melody, haunting and deep, ancient music of Andalusia—the land of *duende*.

The young man starts to dance round and round the chapter room like a burning wheel: a bucket of fire spinning around, carrying monks and benches and windows in its heart.

Like a tide turning, Inman sweeps around in the direction of the west door…and flows out of the room, into the long cloister and its pebbled floor.

The monks listen to the sound of dancer's shoes fading away…softer, fainter, quieter…

Until, finally, *silence*.

In the chapter room, nobody moves.

Click.

The tape recorder snaps off on its own, sending a sharp echo springing off the stone walls.

The silence is dense, tearing the air.

One of the monks leans over to his neighbor and whispers, "*That means that Father Ludovicus is not coming back.*"

Six days later, with head lowered, the abbot walks slowly into the monastic refectory during the midday meal. He says, "Brothers, I just received a telegram. Father Ludovicus is dead. The telegram gives no further information."

After his dance, Inman had disappeared, leaving a note for Br. Simon on the reception desk. After hearing the news about Fr. Ludovicus, Simon felt impelled to rush to his room to reread the note that, originally, he had not understood.

Sorry I had to leave without saying goodbye, dear Brother. You will always be a blessing to me—now, and in our celestial home. When you reach the ocean, I'll be there, waiting for you.

With a deep bow of love, gratitude, and respect,

Inman

A few days later, a shaken Br. Simon enters the abbot's office.

"Do you remember what Inman said, in the chapter room, about seeing Father Ludovicus soon?"

"Vaguely."

"And the letter he left on my desk after departing, do you recall what it said?"

"Not at all."

Simon sits down. His hands are trembling. He reads the letter to the abbot.

"I have no doubt about it. You'll think me crazy for saying what I am about to say, but I must say it."

"Go ahead, Simon."

"I've put together the letter, plus his remark in the chapter room about seeing Ludovicus soon, and what he said about waiting for me when I reached the ocean—meaning when I die—and my overall impression of Inman from our talks. Now I *know* who he is. *I'm sure of it.*"

"What do you mean, you know who Inman is? We *all* know who Inman is."

"Everyone sees the outer form of an extraordinary young man. But nobody sees the *real* Inman...."

The old monk falls silent.

"What are you talking about, Simon?"

"Before God, I am telling you that I am absolutely sure of who Inman is."

The abbot leans forward from his chair, "All right, then, Brother. Tell me, who *is* Inman?"

"The angel of death," Simon half-whispers.

Inman is the angel of death.

Seeing through Our Thoughts

The mind is continually contracting around its
contents. Moment by moment, we are identifying
who we are with what is floating in the mind,
seldom noticing the space in which it floats....When
we become lost, thinking that object "me," it
becomes our predominant reality. It is the loss of
context that causes pain in our lives, that causes the
feeling of confusion and bewilderment that we so
often feel. We don't know who we are or where
we're going because our whole world is mind.

—Stephen Levine

The desert father Evagrius honored the calculating, reasoning
mind that helps us to function in daily life. But he cautioned
against the barrage of thoughts, phrases, and fragments of sentences that whirled around inside the mind—a chaotic multi-
tude that hid our permanent identity: an interior vastness in
which you might travel for months and years and find no one
but Christ.

The desert fathers defined their essential task as dealing
with these thoughts, and with *pathos*—a deeply ingrained tendency to obsess. They were aware of the damage caused by what
the writer Martin Laird has depicted as videos played in the

background of the mind—obsessive, unceasing, negative commentaries.

The desert fathers remembered that Jesus had not confronted the demons in the wilderness directly. Rather, he chose to quote Scripture. The desert fathers went and did likewise, by praying the Jesus Prayer as a way of combating the mind's obsessive running in tight circles. From the beginning, this prayer consisted only of the word *Jesus*, accompanied by the breath.

Over time, the prayer degenerated from simplicity to complexity. First, there was *Jesus*, then *Lord Jesus*, then *Lord Jesus Christ*, then *Son of God*, then *the Son of the Living God*, then *have mercy on me*. The Russians were the last to add to this complexity by adding *a sinner*.

Oblivio, "oblivion": this is what the desert fathers called the state or disposition of being mentally and/or emotionally *elsewhere*. The opposite of oblivion was *memoria*, or "mindfulness": lucidity; a gentle settling into the moment, a wakeful preference for contact with things as they really are—as opposed to slumbering inside the *what if* of the future or the *what was* of the past.

What the desert fathers called *nepsis*, "vigilance"—a clear awareness of thinking—is essential if we are to cultivate *memoria*. Should we get lost in mental wanderings, we "fall asleep." We get "taken for a ride" by one thought after another. If we were to follow a pattern of being swept away by thoughts, eventually we might come to believe that "I am my thoughts": a collapse into identification with what is impermanent.

However, to say, "*I am my thoughts*," would carry the further danger of concluding that "I am my conviction that my value and identity depend on what I accomplish, and on what others think of me."

This may lead to a game of the highest absurdity, in which

I would be looking for approval from the eyes of strangers, while those eyes would be looking to mine for approval!

The writer Eckhart Tolle warns that identification with our mind creates an opaque screen of concepts, labels, images, words, judgments, and definitions that block all true relationships.

Stillness of the body is a great aid to inner vigilance.

A thought is afflictive when it fails to sustain or increase life, and weakens it. These thoughts may look ferocious, but in reality they are shy. They don't like to be watched. Often, they vanish when they sense that they are the focus of attention.

The hospice worker and writer Stephen Levine cautions us to be careful to relate *to* an afflictive thought, rather than *from within it*. If we act from inside, we risk getting entangled in its "bowels."

According to Scripture, to name a person, situation, or thing is to have power over it. When we name an afflictive thought twice, its strength weakens, or vanishes. For example, if we feel an impulse to judge, we say—usually internally— "Judging, judging."

Asking the afflictive thought a question strengthens the internal boundary between us and the thought. "You are over there, on the other side of the boundary; and I am here, on this side, continuing to be who I am."

We may befriend afflictive thoughts and feelings that appear at our inner door, welcoming them with courtesy and respect, as we would a guest, "Would you like some tea?"

This means *being with the thought or thoughts.*

We may ask, "What message might you be bringing me?"

We may even give a name to our thought or mood: Maude, Barsanuphius....

Two familiar practices help to develop not only vigilance, but interior silence as well. In the first practice, we close the eyes and listen to our thoughts. We will notice that inevitably a silent space separates one thought from another. When this happens, we allow our attention to flow quietly into the silence of that open space, and rest there.

When another thought appears, we will be "escorted out" of that space, in a gentle way. Then we wait for the next space between thoughts, and its invitation to "come in." We enter and stay until invited to leave.

In the second practice, internally, we count the breath in a soft, gentle tone of voice. Inhaling, we count "one." Exhaling, we count "two," all the way to ten. Then we return to "one" on the inhalation, "two" on the exhalation. If distracted to the point that we are no longer focused on counting, we return to "one."

Continue either of these practices for as long as you, and the Spirit, would have it.

You may recall what the Selishter Rebbe said: "Be careful with words....They beget either demons or angels. It's up to you to give life to one or another. Be careful, I tell you...."

Be sure that you know what you want to beget. Some don't really want to give up gossip or judging or self-condemnation.

If you are serious about inner transformation, the Spirit will make sure that the light of discernment is not sealed from your eyes.

Ease your breath out, and watch the birth of a new angel!

All I Ask Is that You Listen

When I ask you to listen to me, and you start giving advice, you have not done what I asked.

When I ask you to listen to me, and you begin to tell me why I shouldn't feel that way, you are trampling on my feelings.

When I ask you to listen to me, and you feel you have to do something to solve my problems, you have failed me, strange as that may seem.

Listen! All I ask is that you listen. Not talk or do—just hear me. I can do for myself; I'm not helpless—maybe discouraged and faltering, but not helpless.

When you do something for me that I can and need to do for myself, you contribute to my fear and weakness.

But when you accept as a simple fact that I do feel what I feel, no matter how irrational, then I quit trying to convince you and get about the business of understanding what's behind this irrational feeling.

And when that's clear, the answers are obvious and I don't need advice.

So please listen and just hear me. If you want to talk, wait a minute for your turn, and I'll listen to you.

—Anonymous

CHAPTER 1

A Blessing or a Curse

Everyone
Is God speaking.
Why not be polite and
Listen to
Him?

—The poet, Haviz

The following image pursues Jean Vanier. One day near nightfall, he finds forty children with severe disabilities packed into a small room. Nobody is crying. Vanier wonders, why no tears?

Then he realizes that they are depressed. He remembers that you cry out only if there is hope of being heard. But when there is no hope, you fall into depression.

The children are far too young and too broken to trust the line prayed in the dark by monks, in their final gathering for prayer: "The Lord hears me whenever I call to him."

Whenever.

The ancient Hebrew word for "to bless" means "to honor some important person," or "to bend the knee": not as an act of worship, but as a gesture of reverence toward the inherent nobility of the one blessed. It is to fold the hands before the heart and offer *Namaste*.

But how could the children Jean Vanier saw be aware of their essential beauty, when they had been driven for so long to wander in single file, eyes to the earth, and without a destination, over the barren, frozen fields of winter?

The Hebrew word *qalal*, "to curse," means literally "to make light, to dishonor, to discount": to convey to someone that "you don't count." Or, "You are not worthy of living." A particularly strong discount might transmit the message that "you do not exist"—or "there was never a *you* to begin with." Sometimes the reaction to this message explodes upwards from a dark vault, in the unconscious world. The reaction is as ancient as it is fierce. It is triggered by an imprint encoded in prehistoric times, when persons were forced to battle a threat to their lives. Discounting threatens to annihilate our existence.

Years ago, I met Jacqui Lee Schiff, a psychotherapist, who helped to rehabilitate schizophrenics. Over time, Dr. Schiff noticed something that all her patients had in common. As children, they had been cursed—consistently discounted. They came to sense that their needs, thoughts, and feelings were not worth listening to. "I feel sad, and my father shakes his head and says, how can you feel sad on such a beautiful day? I say that I'm being bullied at school and mother says you're making that up."

Under these circumstances, a child predisposed to schizophrenia gradually arrives at the terrifying nonverbal conclusion that if the "godlike giants" in her life are making no effort to understand her experience, then she must not exist. As a defense against the traumatic prospect of nonexistence, the child withdraws into a strange, unlit world inside, where she responds not to what is, but to fantasy. She feels acute loneliness, split off and disconnected from others, bereft of the blessing that affirms, "You are important. You count. I respect and honor you."

The renowned psychiatrist Karl Menninger confirmed Dr. Schiff's findings when, following decades of work, he said that the experience of not being listened to made people unwell; while the experience of being loved through listening made them well again. Menninger went on to say that the experience of stillness in the presence of another person gave them a sense of their God-given purpose in life.

It's worth noting that, when the Jesuits were preparing to relocate their scholasticate to St. Louis University, they consulted the Menninger Psychiatric Clinic. Uppermost in their mind was, "Of all the elements necessary to maintain the emotional health of a scholastic, which would you specify as most essential?"

The answer, "He would need at least one friend who would listen to him unconditionally; someone who would do everything possible to help him to feel understood."

Affirmation is a way to make clear that one has listened deeply and sincerely, with reverence. "To affirm" derives from the Latin *firmare*, "to strengthen."

The writer Gary Zukav recalls a time when students at the local high school in his hometown are attending a special retreat. The freshmen are welcomed. On the second day, they gather in circles of ten or twelve. Each one writes on a small piece of paper a basic value he or she has recognized in another student—something as meaningful as, "I appreciate the way he respects people by listening well."

Sometime later, a graduate of the high school dies in a traffic accident. In his wallet are pieces of paper with words of appreciation, written by new friends in a circle of peers at that special retreat.

Gary Zukav wonders what words would be so meaningful that someone would carry them with him unto death. He feels that "only a message from the heart can reach that deep, heal that powerfully, and last that long."

Gary Zukav asks his readers, *"How many messages from your heart have you shared today?"**

---

* Gary Zukav, *Soul to Soul: Communications from the Heart* (New York: Free Press, 2008), 22–23.

CHAPTER 2

Faces

Far off in the defenseless years,
so utterly without heat or cold,
an endlessly deep wondering eye stood there
in the night and wept...

—Harry Martinson

"I must tell you...that when I close my eyes, I see faces..."

"Whose faces, Bon Père?"

"*Faces from the Great War*. Faces of terrified soldiers as we awaited an attack of German forces four times greater than our own. Faces of men sitting around after battle like bits of stone, in a daze, or half mad. Or completely gone."

A half-blind Belgian relative, affectionately known as "Bon Père," told me this. Before traveling to Switzerland for six more months of "insults," I accepted his invitation to visit. I will always cherish the graces of that stay.

◊

The morning after my arrival at Bon Père's Belgian home, I wake up around five. At six, the bells in the tower of an ancient church ring the *Angelus*. I take that as a sign that it's time to pray.

I do—by gazing at the stars drifting above my bedroom window. Later my thoughts drift to my hometown of New Orleans, and the old market in the French Quarter where at

Christmas time you can get sweet satsumas, twenty cents a dozen, and snow japonica and Christmas poinsettia.

I walk down a corridor to the French doors that open onto a small patio. Bon Père is sitting on a blue wing chair staring into the shadows. He asks if I would like to talk a bit. I get the impression that he finds my nod uncertain, so I assure him that I do.

After an hour, Bon Père turns his face away from me and gazes at the flowerbed. Two minutes go by, five, six...seven...my palms are moist. *Should I go back to my room?*

After the seventh minute, Bon Père looks at me. He is trying to say something with his eyes, but I can't break the code.

Deep inside his psyche, Bon Père sees the face of a young German soldier whom he has captured. The German soldier asks if he might show Bon Père something. It's in one of his pockets. May he pull it out? "Yes, go ahead." It's a photo of his wife and two small children. They are smiling. He points to his wife, Maria, and the boys, Dietrich and Hans. His eyes are pleading with Bon Père to spare him, for the sake of his family.

"He seemed to be a gentle soul," Bon Père said, "perhaps a Bavarian kid who was forced to enlist. How could I kill someone with a wife and two kids? The questions pounded inside my skull. In the end, I released him."

To show my support, I touch his shoulder. His heart slams in his throat.

"Please, don't do that again. You mean well, but..."

I don't know what to do. Should I urge him to keep telling me what he remembers? Or is it best to distract him away from the memories? I wonder how often he has spoken with someone about the images that haunt him. Perhaps he prefers to talk about them to someone like me, a relative he does not know well.

I pray to the Holy Spirit for guidance, and thank Jesus for the good he will bring out of this situation.

In my naïveté, I wonder, how is it possible that a man could have lived so long and still be haunted by what happened so many years ago?

I sense that Someone is here, listening to what we are thinking and feeling.

A message passes through the silence and settles somewhere inside me. It says, in essence, "*Listen*. Listen thoroughly, listen deep. Let Bon Père feel heard. Let him sense that you care about him and are taking him seriously."

○

"In seventh grade," Bon Père says, "a Sister befriended me. She told me that whenever I felt intense suffering, this pain would help me to connect with what Christ went through in his passion. She said that the pain would help me to get inside that passion and, because of that, touch many, many souls."

He emphasizes that the Sister had said that it was better to say *the* pain, rather than *my* pain.

"When you do that," she told me, "you connect with people who are suffering just as you are."

○

Bon Père says that it took him thirty years to finally revisit the trenches, which had been preserved by the government. He had been told that his trench was among them. His niece persuaded him to go.

"It will help you to heal the memories," she said.

"When I got to the site, I showed my veteran's card, and began to walk toward the trenches. With each passing second, I picked up the pace, and started to run toward them…"

He tried to catch his breath before continuing.

"I stood still. There it was—*my trench*—staring up at me. I was terrified. I remembered the stench and the perennial question: What to do with the dead bodies once the firing had ceased? Bury them? But *where*? We were enslaved to space: a few yards to the front and to the back, a bit more in between the walls."

Bon Père closes his eyes.

It's time to go to my room.

An hour later, there was a knock at the door.

"I wanted to thank you for listening," Bon Père says. "May God bless you for taking this old man seriously. Do you know what? I felt that Jesus was listening through you. *Really, I did.*"

He holds me tight, then lets go. Bon Père turns around slowly and leaves the room, reluctantly.

I sit down, listen to the silence, and pray for—with—Bon Père. I sense that somehow good things will happen in his life: perhaps here, in Belgium, but certainly after he crosses the line into the other world.

Isn't that right, Lord?

I read a passage from Elie Wiesel, who as a teenager had suffered in a Nazi death camp: "*I hear a voice within me telling me to stop mourning the past. I too, want to sing of love and its magic.*"*

Did you hear that, Bon Père?

---

* Elie Wiesel, *The Kingdom of Memory: Reminiscences* (New York: Schocken, 1995), 3.

CHAPTER 3

An Image of Hope

No one has the right to sit down and feel hopeless.
There's too much to do.

—Dorothy Day

Munich, a month after the end of the Second Great War.

Past closing time, a young man is still at his table, staring down into an empty coffee cup. His waitress is too shy to ask him to leave. But Kiara, a second waitress, volunteers to go over to him; not to send him home, but to reach out to the man. She senses the pain he is feeling. She sees it in his eyes.

At the table, she smiles.

"May I join you for a minute or two?"

Her voice is gentle and kind.

"For more than that, if you would like."

During their conversation, Kiara asks, "May I tell you something about myself?"

"Of course."

The waitress starts off by saying that, when she was a child, she learned that to be alone meant that something was wrong.

"As punishment, my father sent me to my room. At school, a teacher ordered me to stand in a corner if I did not meet his expectations. As a teenager, I wanted to go to a movie, but my friends were busy. So I stayed at home, realizing that everyone would stare if I sat in the theatre alone. And of course, as an adult, if I dared to be at a table alone in a restaurant, customers would whisper, 'Poor girl, all by herself. I wonder what is wrong.'"

Kiara asks, "You are alone. May I ask *you*...is something wrong?"

Hans von Scheiding bends his head and begins to trace something on the tablecloth with his index finger. He stops when his hand starts to tremble.

"Illness?"

"No. Nerves."

"Because of the war?"

"Of course."

"The western front—is that where you were?"

"No. Russia."

"Stalingrad?"

"Yes."

Hans starts to unburden. The charred memories of the siege of Stalingrad imprison him. His nights? Shaken by nightmares. Weary of living? No. He has ceased to live.

Kiara tries to help him: Why not try this...or that...?

Hans backs away from each suggestion. But she persists.

"*I know!* The circus! Go while it is still on the outskirts of the city. Come Monday it will be gone. Lose yourself in the crowd. Watch the clown. Listen to his jokes. Laugh!"

"That won't work, either."

"Why?"

"*Because I am the clown.*"

◊

Hans von Scheiding knew that aloneness was not a sign of weakness or trouble. He simply had to have time to sort things out by himself. Sitting in a restaurant after closing time was another way to do that.

"You are fortunate," Kiara said, after hearing more of his story. "Fortunate in that your father was a kind and mature man, faithful to the true—and not Nazi—values of our Fatherland. God protected you from the violence of the traditional, unquestioned German version of child rearing. Had you been traumatized as a boy, you would never have allowed me to be with you. So I assume that your father was not a violent man."

"He is a beautiful person," Hans said. "He refused to bend me into blind obedience. My father supported the White Rose, the student movement that tried to sway the youth away from Nazism."

Now Hans resembled one of the young men of the desert fathers' era. Each evening, their custom was to bring to an elder the story of what had mattered in their lives during the day, especially significant thoughts. The elder would listen with respect, and then speak a word of wisdom.

Kiara's word of wisdom was a gesture: her heart gazing with compassion into innocent eyes. As the night unfolded, she reached deeper into his wounds. Kiara listened with a gentle spirit, saying without saying, "Yes, I hear you. Yes, I understand. Yes, Hans, I'm for you and with you."

After much listening, it became clear to Kiara that Hans had fallen into the hopeless trap of believing that his agony would last forever. He was locked up in an endless *now*. In a variety of ways, she asked him to ponder the possibility that he was not yet seeing the total picture; that he was assuming that the way he felt would *always* be the way he felt.

She challenged him to use his imagination to see that his situation was not a cause for despair.

"Everything has a beginning and an end," Kiara said. "Even if you were not to see an end to the darkness in this world, you would in the next."

The psychiatrist Viktor Frankl, who endured the trauma of a Nazi death camp, tells us about a common element in the survival of the prisoners: their capacity to hope, to see beyond the edges of the present moment. He recalls a man who dreamed that the camp would be liberated by March 31, 1945. From that point on, life had meaning, filled with hope. He lived for March 31, believed in it. The man thought that on April 1 he would be raising a glass of wine gallantly, after praying *kaddish*: the prayer for the dead.

March 31 came…and nothing happened: the same guards, the same stench, the same lice. In the piercing evening air, he died—to all appearances, of typhus. When the dream proved to be no more than that, the man's resistance to a latent infection had collapsed. He lost all hope and his desire to live.

In times of crisis, it is essential to find one's version of Kiara: someone willing to listen deeply; a trusted friend capable of bringing into focus a broad picture, or context: "There is a beginning to your pain, and an end."

Without this wider picture, time becomes a captor. Where context is missing, so is meaning. Then life appears bleak, "too much to deal with": a series of random, disconnected events, with no unifying purpose. But to be without purpose is to risk watching one's life slide gradually from dread to despair.

CHAPTER 4

A Blessing in Winter

I feel myself swelling and aching
in a hundred places,
above all in the depths of my heart.
> —Rainer Maria Rilke

A monastic community informs one of its members, "It's nearly unanimous. We are going to vote you in as abbot."

At a meeting two weeks prior to the abbatial election, the monk announces, "Now, all I can do is hope that the second coming will get here before the election."

An abbot consoles him, "The day I was elected abbot was the most depressing of my life. When the abbot general called to confirm the election, he asked how I felt. I said, 'Empty.' He thought this was marvelous, that now God would work more through my emptiness than through my gifts."

◊

Here emptiness is not an experience of being adrift or disconnected from others, nor is it self-pity or depression.

This emptiness is a healthy sense of incompletion. It reassures a person, "You are content and at peace in your life. And yet something is missing: the fullness that awaits you after death."

If incompletion is not understood and stays at an unconscious level, it can be dangerous. What if someone were to connect this experience to the wrong source? What if one were to feel that something is terribly wrong because he has yet to "get to the top," or because he married the wrong woman?

It might happen that during our odyssey, something may go wrong and sadness, turmoil, and dissatisfaction set in. Many years ago, while at another monastery, I found a piece of paper tucked inside the pages of a book. It was written in meticulous Gothic script: *Ruttity, ruttity, rut, rut, rut. Same old monastic tedium.*

I knew who wrote that way: a gentle and generous monk, who each evening liked to walk through the unworried forest, pondering and praying: Fr. Daniel.

A Brother caught in crisis may wonder if he should leave the monastery. Perhaps he should, following a thorough and honest process of discernment with someone he trusts.

This process would invite the Brother to hold still, to pray, to ponder and discern further. Give it time.

The same might be said of a relationship in crisis, or a troubled marriage.

A few years ago, I was in the office of Abbot Seraphim. We talked about the not-so-recent departures of Brothers W, X, and Y. We talked, too, about sixty-seven-year-old Br. Zachary, the prior.

Walking among ferns in the forest one afternoon, this monk told the abbot that he was leaving. His jaw hanging down, Br. Zachary turned his face toward a cottonwood tree and wept. The stunned abbot sensed much darkness beneath his feet.

"But…*why?*"

The Brother's lips quivered.

"I can't put it into words. I know, I know....I've kept so much to myself. *Too much.* It's too late to turn around."

"But at your age..."

"I know, I know. I've made up my mind."

"But you haven't discerned with me....Have you, with *anyone*?"

No answer.

"And how would you support yourself, at your age?"

At your age—again, Zachary thought. He had heard that phrase as an adolescent, and now here, in his sixties. It seemed clear that Brother's heart had walked into a great night of crisis and confusion.

Around midnight a week later, Br. Zachary left the monastery, making sure that no one saw him slip past the front gate.

I wondered what would have happened, had Brother stayed and waited in the darkness just a while longer.

Or a good bit longer.

"That's the secret," the abbot says. "Be with the darkness, wait it out, as long as it takes...and see what happens."

The abbot recalled a time when he was bereft of energy, or of the slightest enthusiasm. Everything seemed flat, sterile. He had trouble sleeping and had lost his appetite.

Feeling powerless to deal with this desert experience, Fr. Seraphim questioned whether he was in the right place. He wondered if he should make himself *do something*; maybe get more involved in some social cause—surely that was needed in the world. Or he might try to make new friends, or start a new industry in the monastery, or take up a hobby, go hunting, watch movies—without anyone knowing about it, of course!

Standing back from all these options, it occurred to Seraphim that none of them would be enough to snap him out of his ever-deepening darkness.

"I'm sinking fast," he thought, "and I have to do something about it! *What about marriage?* Surely that would do it....Or *would* it?"

"It was a heavy, searing loneliness," Seraphim said. "I could have filled up the emptiness through the many available diversions. But I said no, I'm going to wait this out. And I did, until somehow grace broke through to show me the meaning of this ordeal."

Gradually, the great darkness drove Seraphim into the truth about himself, things he had not dared to admit until now.

"A kind of plague breaks out in the heart as one discovers aspects of one's reality that are highly disconcerting," Fr. Matthew Kelty says.

Seraphim had taken a vow of *obedience*, a word derived from the Latin *ob-audire*, "to listen thoroughly and deeply" to God, to others, to the circumstances of his life, and even to the kind of plague that erupts in the heart, and brings us to our knees.

Seraphim had taken a vow of stability: a solemn promise to hold still and to look steadily into the eyes of truth. Seraphim listened to himself and held still until he admitted that he craved power.

"That's why I wanted to be abbot," he said. "I relished the power that came with the office."

Seraphim admitted that whenever a Brother said that he was leaving, his concern was not about the monk, but around a question: "Who will replace him in his job?" Seraphim read only to find material for his conferences with the monks.

Once the door opens to truth, it tends to stay open, at least for a while. Other insights wander onto the scene. In tune with the breath of the Spirit, they are met with a mindful presence: a simple resting in each insight.

Seraphim's self-knowledge was worth waiting for: a blessing, after a winter of desolation.

He had not realized that the room that was his life had been full of the scent of incense. Jasmine.

He remembered alternation of experience and realized that he had embraced it once again. He had heard footsteps inside moving toward him to say that no matter how painful the sudden, unexpected eruption of self-knowledge might be, it was essential that he face it.

CHAPTER 5

Faith Is Fire, Not Sediment

(The Baal Shem Tov taught that) faith was fire, not
sediment. Did not a pillar of fire serve as a guide
when the people Israel roamed in the wilderness?
And fire was the beginning of light.

—Abraham Heschel

Abraham may have played a significant role in the Jewish
Scriptures, but as a child, the thought of him terrified the future
writer Nikos Kazantzakis. He would hide behind his desk for
fear that Abraham would find him and carry him off blindfolded,
perhaps to a smoldering plain where earthly spirits lived.

Legend has it that one day his teacher said, "Just keep the
commandments, lad, and you're sure to go to Abraham's
bosom." That was enough to convince Kazantzakis that he must
never, ever keep the commandments.

But we may find an element of truth in his description of
Abraham. The sound of his name did come from far away, as
though from some deep well: the silence of the Great Blue
Heron.

Hebrew Tradition identifies "all that I am" with the name,
so when God changed Abram's name to Abraham, it marked a
turning point in the old man's life: his surrender to a Sacred
Destiny. It meant that he was ready to begin an odyssey that
would lead him into the unknown reaches of a wilderness

where, like John the Baptist centuries later, he would learn the language of God.

Abraham was seventy-five when his Friend asked him to leave his country, his kinfolk, and his father's home to trek through large, barren spaces—but not only, or primarily, through geographical spaces.

In the Book of Genesis, God tells Abraham to go forth (*lech lecha*) from his land.

Rabbi Rami Shapiro points out that the Hebrew *lech lecha* is usually translated as "go forth." This translation isn't wrong, just flat. True, Abram and Sarai are going to physically leave home, but the Hebrew suggests that their journey is as much a spiritual one as it is a physical one. *Lech lecha* means "Walk toward yourself."*

This is reminiscent of the most basic "slogan" of the desert fathers and mothers: *redite ad cor*, "return to the heart"—the second heart, whose name is Narnia within Narnia.

God is saying, "My dear Abraham, I'm calling you to live with gentleness. I'm inviting you to experience me and others at a level beyond words, concepts, or feelings and, at the same time, to express that living through words and concepts and feelings. Do you understand, Abraham, my brother? The kernel and its shell, *together!*"

Some have trouble choosing to leave behind the cultural conviction that "my value and identity depend on what I do and what others think of me."

Fr. Matthew Kelty recalls that, some years ago, a young man, who had been a semiprofessional dancer and actor, entered

---

* Rabbi Rami Shapiro, "There Is No Password," in *Kid Spirit Online-The Nature of Truth*, January 21, 2014, http://kidspiritonline.com/2014/01/there-is-no-password/.

the Abbey of Gethsemani. Eventually, he left. He had to. Later, he told Matthew why.

I was always on stage. You know, since I was a small child I have always been called on to sing some song, to do a little dance, and that continued all my life. I developed early on an awareness of people watching me, applauding me, making much of me. Now it seems part of me. And so here at Gethsemani.

All the more with the liturgy, ritual, costume, and other dramatic aspects. I could not shake myself of an audience, real or imagined.

Try as I would, it stayed with me and ruined the place, the life for me. And so, I had to leave.

Beginning with Abraham, the father of believers, a pattern emerges: a consistent rhythm of pilgrimage. In the next generation, Isaac leaves his mother, and after him, Jacob departs from Beersheba. In the next generation, Joseph leaves for Egypt, and later Moses forsakes Egypt and leads the Jewish people into the wilderness.

One by one, pilgrims are sent into the darkness of unknown lands. They leave with gladness and deep song: Isaiah, Baruch, Ezekiel, Daniel, Hosea....

And Habakkuk.

We know little about Habakkuk—only that his name derives from a Hebrew word meaning "fruit tree," or "plant"; and that he was asked to go on a mission to Daniel in the lion's den. His contribution to the Jewish Scriptures is minimal if we judge in terms of length; Habakkuk's prophecy fills barely a couple of pages.

His best-known aphorism is "we live by faith"—the way a plant lives by the sap that flows through its stalk.

Habakkuk was another ancient figure whose imaginary presence terrified Nikos Kazantzakis. When he first heard the prophet's name in grammar school, he reacted as vehemently as he had to the "specter" of Abraham. Responding to inner fantasy, the child was sure that Habakkuk was a "bogeyman," prowling around in the shadows of a courtyard at night. But, as with his delusions about Abraham, even this description of Habakkuk holds some truth.

The shadows in the courtyard are real, but they are not the cloak of Habakkuk prowling around in the moonlight. "Yahweh is our shadow," a spiritual master says somewhere: the Great Blue Heron accompanies us everywhere with gentle strength, whether we walk or eat—or run, like a child fleeing from the hand of an imaginary prophet.

When Habakkuk says, "We live by faith," he means that we surrender to an Invisible Presence: a yielding to a gentle hand, which reaches out from inside a Great Round Dance. Habakkuk's faith is an even vision that experiences a Great Silence behind every circumstance and event: the Formless under so many forms.

Faith is *aman*—"firm, solid"—and *emet*—"fidelity," the sister of *hesed*: the unconditional love-energy promised by the Secret One to "the father of believers," the holy pilgrim, Abraham.

Habakkuk's faith matched that of St. Paul, who knew that nothing—hardship, hunger, death—could separate him from the Great Heart of his beloved Jesus.

Faith is more than an emotional or intellectual assent to Mystery. It is Christ stretching out his hand to Peter in a storm, and Peter yielding to *tarnar*, the Indian word for "savior," which literally means one who "causes us to float."

Faith is fire, not sediment.

CHAPTER 6

A Sacred Song

The vision of peace is about coming out from
behind barriers and discovering people as they are.
The Spirit of God will be given, so that then we will
see people, not through the glasses of our
impoverished humanity and its wounds, but as God
sees them. It's a transformation. And to enter into
the world of transformation we need to want it.

—Jean Vanier

"I know you're an American, but you seem like one of us—
European," a German told me one day long ago. His observation
didn't surprise me. My father was a diplomat from the Walloon
region of Belgium, and my mother a gifted pianist from a long
line of Andalusian families. So the old châteaus along the Meuse
and the snowy trees of the Ardennes forest and the canal of
Bruges are all part of me—and so is the poetry of Lorca, and the
gypsy music of southern Spain.

Part of my European heritage is *canto hondo*: "deep song."

Canto hondo is the ancient music of Andalusia—deeper,
Federico Garcia Lorca says, than all the wells and seas that sur-
round the world, music so old that "it comes from the first sob
and the first kiss." *Canto hondo* is ecstatic, the joy of the
Andalusian who rarely notices the "middle tone," who either
"shouts at the stars or kisses the red dust of the road." This

sacred song is simple, sure and barefooted, bringing some degree of self-respect to hearts unaware of their innate nobility.

Like *canto hondo*, the pilgrim's deep song of faith—a melody he shares with his Secret Friend—is a stranger to the restraint of the "middle tone." A canticle of devotion more ancient than *canto hondo*, it begins beyond time in the silence of our Creator.

God's *canto hondo*, his song of gentle strength, begins in the silence of the Father, flows into the Son, and through the power of the Spirit, streams into the *cantaor*—"the singer." Without leaving the pilgrim-*cantaor*, God's love continues its journey, wandering over the earth's surface, flowing into the deep valleys of the universe, far into the shores of the men and women of this world—all for no other reason than this: "I sing because I sing."

For Lorca, the pilgrim's deep song "rouses ancient essences from their sleep, wraps them in his voice, and flings them into the wind." The pilgrim-*cantaor* is a muse who rouses the buried gardens of his geography, folds them in his voice, and yields them into the gentle hand of a Secret Friend. But each singer rouses ancient essences in his own way, according to the unique gift of his particular calling.

We are in the middle of Lent, and on two consecutive days, Christ's words end the Gospel at Mass on the same note, "I have come to serve." He will say the same thing on Holy Thursday. Christ will kneel and wash the feet of his disciples, and then the Servant will stand up and look at each of us for a long, long moment before saying, "I want you to do the same thing. I long for you to pour yourself into service. I want you to uplift the world with your words, and give birth to angels by your deeds. I yearn that you be *cantaors* on a vast night full of stars, where the tears of blind trees can fall at last...."

But the hermit in the wilderness, someone will say—how can he be a *cantaor*? Far from everyone but the silence of the eider duck sitting on her nest, how can he serve?

Listen to this fragment of an unpublished Syriac hymn by St. Ephraim, in the fifth century:

> He who celebrates alone in the heart of the wilderness,
> He is a great assembly.
> If two together celebrate among the rocks,
> Thousands and tens of thousands are present there.

When the Baal Shem Tov saw that his people were in danger, he did not rush to the market place to comfort them. He went deep into the forest and prayed alone. Then he lit a fire and said a blessing. And the danger passed over his people, and they lived on and grew in faith, like Abraham and Habakkuk.

This is why the hermit, and his fellow pilgrims, can uplift the world without saying a word, and give birth to angels without doing a thing.

CHAPTER 7

The Music that Befriends Us

Author Sue Monk Kidd uses a musical metaphor to
describe the stages of contemplative awareness. In
the first stage...we can hear the words but not the
music; in the next stage, we appreciate both the
words and the music, and in the final stage, we
become the music.

—Liz Hill

Once upon a time, the space known as the French Quarter was
all there was of New Orleans. As a child, I frequented an exu-
berant place in the Quarter called Preservation Hall, where musicians did all they could to preserve the treasures of early jazz.

Sydney Becket was one of them. One night, a man told him
how much it meant to him to hear Becket play, that he'd never
heard sounds like that before. The master of the clarinet and
soprano sax shrugged, "I played as I always have played."

"No, no," the man declared, firmly. "This is *your* music!"

Later, Becket pondered what the man had said and concluded, "No music is *my* music. If you can feel the music, then
it's yours as much as it is mine. To feel the sun, you've got to go
outside and let yourself be *in* it."

To feel the sun, the music, God—you have to be *in* the sun,
in the music, *in* God.

Isn't that what St. Paul concluded? When you come down to it, he said, the only thing that counts is to be *in* God—the Vastness in whom we live and move.

Which means just be who you are, have been, and always will be—*in* God.

To which Becket no doubt would say, in the old fashioned language of New Orleans, "*Yeah, you right!*"

Have you ever stood in front of a tree for a while, allowing your eyes to rest on its texture, when—without expecting it—you sense its aliveness? Then you are *in* the tree! And within minutes it feels as though you and the tree are one, while remaining two?

Have you ever let go *into* music, and felt no separation between yourself and its notes and rhythm?

While hearing or singing sacred music, it may seem that we have been drawn into its center. It's a song with many verses, and yet time passes quickly. Or is it that time as we know it has disappeared?

The Spirit would remind us that at this moment we are sharing Christ's life in a unique way; one that knows nothing of linear time. When temporal veils—which slide between us and what is—are parted, we realize that we have been the song all along.

If we open our inner doors, music will come in and befriend us. In its own way, it will express an eagerness to breathe with the Spirit; and to create a climate in which God might more deeply inhale us into his gentle strength.

The compulsive and controlling ways of the mind are powerless to sidetrack music, since its harmony swims well beneath the intellect.

Music yearns to be our ally. Like a good friend, it does not insist or intrude. It respects our "boundaries." Musical rhythm, tone, harmony—and the subtle emotions it conveys—would never force themselves on us.

If you feel inclined, relax and listen to a piece of music that has impacted you on your journey into God. Listen until it is rooted in your musical memory.

Then it will be your companion during the day, and at night, too. Inside you, it will sing of God through its vibrations, for as long as you like. At other times, it will appear whenever the time is right and leave when your attention turns in a different direction.

At various moments during the day, it will appear as in the Gestalt "figure and ground"—with the music in the background of your heart and mind, while in the foreground you attend to what requires attention.

Change the lyrics of a sacred song if this will render it more personal. Or why not compose your own music?

You may say, "I don't have the talent."

Who told you that?

Years ago, I encouraged a young man to compose. He said the same thing, "I lack talent."

However, he took the matter to prayer and waited a good while before deciding to meet the challenge. Gradually, notes began to stir in his unconscious world and made their way to a space where rhythm unfolded; and lyrics too.

Today he is a professional musician.

Chant differs from modern song in that it consists of a gentle rise in volume up to the midpoint of a musical line then falls without effort, decreasing in volume at the end of the line.

This rise and fall is highly significant. The inhalation up to the midpoint of the line expresses our ascent into God's kindness. Exhaling at the end of the musical line is when we rest in his silence. Here you find no effort to control the ebb and flow between movement and rest. This is the rhythm of chant and of deep prayer. *When was the last time you sang?*

CHAPTER 8

Why Not Become All Fire?

When your household sits down to a meal, if you
are wise, you will sit down yourself, and then you
will be able to serve them easily and happily. In your
charity to your neighbor, remember that your
nearest neighbor is yourself.

—John of Forde

As usual, the Midrash speaks in a direct way, often enough different from the way a story or truth is understood and has been for centuries. An example of this is a Midrash interpretation of a story about Elijah the prophet.

"God wanted me to prophesy in a strong yet respectful way," Elijah says, "but I didn't. I was incapable of kindness."

At the time, Elijah is sure that he is justified in turning against his community—judging, intimidating, terrorizing even to the point of murder...as he did when he slaughtered the false prophets....

When God hears about this, he buries his head in his hands.

"I didn't know what Elijah would do," God says, weeping —*kivyachol*. "He knew that the commandments forbid murder. And yet..."

It's something that all Jews—and most Christians—know. Elijah left this world in a chariot of fire.

In Scripture, "fire" symbolizes purification.

"I needed to be purified by God," Elijah says, "so that I might love the way he loves. Yahweh pulled me up into the heavens because he wanted to rip control out of my hands and make me so very vulnerable."

Elijah says that, to a few, this lifting up in a chariot is equivalent to the ascensions of Jesus and Mary.

"The comparison embarrasses me," Elijah says.

When the fiery chariot reaches its destination, Elijah vanishes from the pages of history. But in time, he starts to reappear in the world. No one can predict when or where. He shows up in myriad ways, in various circumstances.

If he has passed judgment on prostitutes, the unthinkable happens. He appears as a prostitute; if he has been cruel toward women, he appears as a woman; if he has shown disdain for the ritually impure, he appears as a leper.

Elijah does all he can to draw these people closer to the heart of *Yahweh, Blessed Be He.*

No longer the Elijah of old, he does not terrorize or threaten to kill if someone refuses to think as he does. Instead, he encourages everyone to see in a new and timeless light: to feel at least a fleeting touch of *things as they really are, and of God as he really is.*

But fire also symbolizes what St. John of the Cross speaks of in his work "The Living Flame of Love."

Here is a story, from the desert fathers' tradition:

A young man hesitated to see Abba Evaristus because he did not want to bother the great desert father with his "issues." When he heard about this, he said, "When tempted to speak ill of another, that's the time to bar the door of our lips, but not to shut the door to our dwelling."

Silence, moonlight.

Zacharias knocks at the door of Abba Evaristus's dwelling. The old man bids him enter. Except for a couple of chairs, a desk, and a mat on the floor, the place is barren. The tiny place of prayer has merged with the silence of the wilderness outside.

The young man's face is pale, drawn. He yearns to come to new life with the help of Evaristus.

"Things have not worked out as I planned," Zacharias admits. "My expectations, struggles, achievements in the city—for *what*?"

He carries an unbearable loneliness.

After all he has heard about Evaristus, he does not expect the old man to react the way his indifferent father would: pressing his lips together for a moment, letting out a deep sigh of frustration, along with a slight shaking of the head. Instead, Evaristus smiles. He nods, "Go on, my son, continue. I'm listening."

There follows a monologue for close to an hour. Zacharias ends by saying that to get out of his darkness he has fasted, a lot. And yet, nothing! There is just a hollow feeling, which feels like grief, in the pit of the stomach. He knows that he must go deeper, but does not know how.

"I'm exhausted," he says. "What else can I do?"

The desert father closes his eyes and does not speak.

A minute passes, three, six. Fear cuts through Zacharias, *What's going on? Why is he just sitting there?*

Evaristus stands up. Very slowly, he raises his hands to the heavens. His fingertips become ten lanterns of fire.

Then, the words: "Why...not...become...all...fire?"

A wall of darkness gets up and moves. It opens the roof, darts into the friendly sky, and disappears.

All that remains in Zacharias is a gentleness not of this world.

CHAPTER 9

The Secret

Beneath the waters, since I was a boy,
I have dreamt of strange and dark treasures,
Not of gold, or strange stones, but the true
Gift, beneath the pale lakes of Minnesota.

—Robert Bly

When you're ten—and it happens on a New England beach in the heart of summer—you keep a secret, a story which will take years to tell, to more than just a few.

Here it is.

Deep into an afternoon's fourth hour, a shroud of mist hovers over the beach as I enter the rough waters. I swim fast, knowing I am going further out than I should. When a lifeguard notices, he shouts through a megaphone, *"Hey kid, what are you DOING? Come back—NOW!"*

It's too late. I'm caught in a riptide.

I drown.

Down there, desperation. I fight to cough up the salty water. The relentless flooding of nostrils and lungs continues.

I am pulled up to the surface. I catch sight of the lifeguard, swimming toward me at high speed. He is a good distance away. I sink again.

There's more flooding of nostrils and lungs. The desperation grows worse.

A second ascension. The lifeguard is closer, but not close enough.

I go down again. The water is tenacious, and I'm tiring, badly. All of a sudden everything goes black. Now I am resting deep inside a serenity that is impossible to describe. The water has become my friend.

For a long time, I remember nothing beyond that.

Most children who have near death experiences hide what happened. And so I, a ten-year-old, keep my secret to myself.

But one afternoon, I disclose my experience to a doctor. He says, rather matter-of-fact, "It's impossible for a child to feel an enormous level of fear, panic, and pain one moment, and the next to be at peace. It just doesn't happen that way. Nor is it possible for anyone to float around under water for any length of time and still be alive. *You were dead.* The serenity you felt was, I feel sure, the kind of peace found in the other world."

Later that afternoon, a sturdy, almost intimidating friend of the family becomes angry when I tell her what the doctor said.

"Don't you *ever* say a word about that to your family or to anyone else! I was there, on the beach, when you started to have trouble in the water. *Trouble.* Nothing else. Do you understand?"

I nod my head.

"OK."

So I keep the secret to myself.

A memory. I am fifteen, alone in a car, waiting for friends to arrive. Abruptly, the word *service* invites itself into my awareness. The word is magical. I feel spacious and quiet.

After that, each time I hear or think or read about the word *service*, I am transported into an enchanted inner world, where you hear not even a murmur of conversation.

A few years before entering the monastery, I was driving across the longest bridge in America. A scene nudges its way to the surface of my awareness.

My body is a body of light. I can think, feel, listen, and see. I am in the midst of an enormous Light. I see no hands, no feet, no eyes, no ears, and yet I feel the tenderness of Someone holding me gently, in a way I have never known. The silence of the Light is powerful.

It communicates with me, through thought transference, "You're going back. A mission is waiting for you."

I'm ten. I don't understand. I ask, "What does this mean?"

"*It's simple. Your mission is to serve.*"

When I hear that, I still don't get it.

I get it now, and have for many years. The slopes of my heart have grown. Their edges are clearer and livelier than when I was a child of ten. I understand the message of the Being of Light.

It's midafternoon at the monastery.

I feel it coming.

I open the chapter room door leading into the rock garden and walk to the almond tree. The fresh air feels good.

Sensing a presence behind me, I turn around. It's a Stranger, with radiant eyes. He asks, "In your lifetime, have you done your best to beget angels by your deeds?"

I have no place to hide.

Scenes from my life begin to race inside me at rapid, almost timeless, speed.

When the scenes stop, he asks, "Well, how was it?"

"How was *what*?"

"The review of your life."

I don't know what to say.

With a slow, gentle gesture, he motions to me to follow him.

"Where are we going?"

"Home. It's time to go home."

I pause beneath the almond tree and look at the hills I love. Snowflakes are falling gently across my face.

Then I turn back to him.

"Now?" I ask, quietly.

"Yes. Now."

I gaze at the high monastery wall and the steeple arching into the sky and follow him home.

Dealing with Afflictive Feelings

> Many of the happiest and most peaceful people I
> know love a God who walks with crucified people,
> and thus reveals and "redeems" their plight as His
> own.
>
> — Richard Rohr

Alice Miller, a German psychotherapist, did not turn her head away from the truth that persons who willfully inflict harm on others are suffering. This pain may take many forms, including self-hatred or repressed rage over abuse, as in the case of German childrearing from the turn of the century.

During that era, German boys were bludgeoned into obeying blindly. Beaten repeatedly, humiliated and abused into submission, they were powerless to ventilate the rage they felt against their fathers. As young men in the SS, Gestapo, *Wehrmacht*, and other military groups, they displaced their wrath onto innocent civilians of occupied countries.

An old relative shared with me the very painful memory of German soldiers occupying his town in Belgium: men who took pleasure in shooting children with "dum-dum" bullets, which ripped open the skin and led to a slow, agonizing death.

Here is a practice with origins in the ancient Eastern Tradition. It helps us to grow in the likeness of Christ by doing as he did when he took to himself the sufferings of wounded people.

First let's construct a scene.

The memory of Devon's fierce verbal assault against you burrows in your mind. It triggers a pull to revenge, as resentment runs recklessly through your body. Your sleep is restless. A few minutes after waking up, you notice that your hands are tightly clenched fists. The day seems to drag on endlessly.

In your head, you try to make peace with Devon, but this gets you nowhere. *Since resentment is lodged in the body, any attempt to reconcile in the head alone doesn't usually work.*

To deal with any afflictive feeling, it is important to be with it *where it is*…in the chest, the stomach, or some other area where a dark and tight feeling might be brooding. It is best to settle into the moment, to be with the feeling.

Anne Sexton was onto something when she wrote, "*Oh, darling, let your body in, let it tie you in.*"*

Before starting the practice, please at least "take it on faith" that Devon is suffering—for whatever reason, just as our resentment is causing *us* to suffer.

There are so many in our world who are also suffering at this moment, some as vengeful as the Germans of *that* era. Or the lad in the yellow pants on the day I was almost killed in a forlorn ghetto long ago.

So this practice is not just for Devon's benefit and yours. *It is also for the benefit of the crucified, wherever they might be.* In a mysterious way, we are mediating God's strength and grace to

---

* Anne Sexton, "Little Girl, My String Bean, My Lovely Woman," in *The Complete Poems: Anne Sexton* (New York: Mariner Books, 1999), 145ff.

innocent people—some of them in agony from torture of a magnitude beyond belief.

In a gesture of trust, express your gratitude to God *in advance*, for bringing life-giving power to you and to Devon through this practice.

Gently whisper to the great and tender heart of Jesus: *Thank you for transforming resentment into compassion and darkness into light.*

At this point, you are ready to make your own Christ's words:

Come to me, you who are heavily burdened, and I will give you quiet. For I am gentle and humble of heart.

Imagine a sphere of white light in the center of your chest. This brightness symbolizes the power inherent in God's image at the inmost level of heart.

Then imagine dark smoke in the center of Devon's chest. It is as though black drapes are hiding the Divine Image within him. The murkiness represents Devon's suffering.

Take in a deep breath from the abdomen, and then exhale into the smoke that is plundering Devon's inner world.

Now imagine that you are breathing the heavy burden of his suffering into the light inside your chest and dissolving the strength of its negativity.

While exhaling, let your light stream back into Devon's darkness. Then inhale more of the suffering of a heart turned to stone. Lead it into the healing light. Send it back....

Exhale again, sensing that God's compassion is flowing through your breath into the heart of Devon's darkness. Inhale more of the murkiness, and see it change into God's light at the center of your chest. Then exhale....

I taught this practice to Jason, a young man who had spent time in our monastery as a long-term guest. When he returned to the city, he got a job. After two weeks, the boss—Mr. Taylor—assaulted him through strong verbal abuse.

Late that afternoon, Jason called his girlfriend to break a date, "I have to be by myself."

In his apartment, the young man felt drummed to battle by a fierce resentment. Its savage energy thrashed in his stomach, causing teeth to clench.

Did the Great Heart inspire him to remember the practice?

He argued with himself, "Should I do this or not?" In the end, he chose to "try it out."

Against the background of light-hearted music, which he had thought might calm him down—but didn't—Jason took a few frail breaths, which slowly swelled in power.

He thanked God for "What you will do..." Then he applied the practice to his circumstances. Gradually, the resentment subsided.

After much practice, long into the night, Jason began to feel quieter. By dawn, he felt grounded.

The next day, he returned to work. Apparently accustomed to the drumbeat of conflict, the boss was sure that the young man would come to work filled with anger, even rage. But instead, it was as though Jason had put a gentle hand over the boss's clenched fist, and wished him peace.

After recollecting himself to the extent possible, Mr. Taylor sat with Jason and asked, "What happened between the time you left the office and entered it a while ago?"

When he heard about the practice, he persuaded Jason to share the details with him.

Mr. Taylor listened carefully as Jason explained. Eventually, he internalized the practice; confident that now he held close to his heart the sacred gift of a "weapon of peace."

"I'm so grateful," he said.

You may apply this practice to yourself.

Should you experience a feeling that oppresses you, observe where it predominates in the body. Breathe in its black smoke and allow the Great Heart to transform that dark energy into life-giving light.

Then send it back to the afflicted area. Continue as usual.